MOVING
ACROSS
DIFFERENCES

MOVING ACROSS DIFFERENCES

HOW STUDENTS ENGAGE LGBTQ+ THEMES
IN A HIGH SCHOOL LITERATURE CLASS

MOLLIE V. BLACKBURN

SUNY
PRESS

Cover art by Mindi Rhoades.

Published by State University of New York Press, Albany

This book is freely available in an open access edition thanks to TOME (Toward an Open Monograph Ecosystem)—a collaboration of the Association of American Universities, the Association of University Presses, and the Association of Research Libraries—and the generous support of The Ohio State University Libraries. Learn more at the TOME website, available at: openmonographs.org.

Printed in the United States of America

For information, contact State University of New York Press, Albany, NY
www.sunypress.edu

Library of Congress Cataloging-in-Publication Data

Name: Blackburn, Mollie V., 1969– author.
Title: Moving across differences : how students engage LGBTQ+ themes in a
   high-school literature class / Mollie V. Blackburn.
Description: Albany : State University of New York Press, [2022] | Includes
   bibliographical references and index.
Identifiers: LCCN 2022005748 | ISBN 9781438490113 (hardcover : alk. paper) |
   ISBN 9781438490120 (ebook) | ISBN 9781438490106 (pbk. : alk. paper)
Subjects: LCSH: American literature—Study and teaching (Secondary) |
   Sexual minorities in literature. | Multicultural education—United States. | Moral
   education—United States.
Classification: LCC PS47.U6 B55 2022 | DDC 810.71/2—dc23/eng/20220621
LC record available at https://lccn.loc.gov/2022005748

10 9 8 7 6 5 4 3 2 1

To my siblings, who have taught me the importance of moving across differences since as long as I can remember. We move across differences to find one another, to connect with one another, over and over again.

Contents

LIST OF ILLUSTRATIONS ix

ACKNOWLEDGMENTS xi

INTRODUCTION
Theoretical, Empirical, and Contextual 1

CHAPTER 1
Moving with Respect to Sexual Diversity in Classroom Encounters 27

CHAPTER 2
Moving with Respect to Gender Diversity in Classroom Encounters 53

CHAPTER 3
Moving with Respect to Racial Diversity in Classroom Encounters 79

CHAPTER 4
Moving with Respect to Religion in Classroom Encounters 113

CHAPTER 5
Moving with Respect to Families in Classroom Encounters 127

CHAPTER 6
Moving, (For)Giving, and Ethical Classroom Encounters 151

CONCLUSION
Moving and Giving toward Ethical Encounters 163

viii | Contents

APPENDIX
Research Methodology   167

REFERENCES   185

INDEX   193

List of Illustrations

Figure 1   Mac's illustration of Felix in Brezenoff's (2011)
           Brooklyn, Burning   63

Table 1   Chart created in the fall 2015 class to characterize traits
           typically associated with men and women   76

Table 2   Units and related reading and writing assignments
           for the spring 2015 course   169

Table 3   Units and related reading and writing assignments
           for the fall 2015 course   172

Table 4   Units and related reading and writing assignments
           for the spring 2016 course   174

Acknowledgments

I am profoundly grateful for and deeply indebted to so many who have supported me, my work, and my family during the years and across the spaces in which this book came to fruition. I strive to acknowledge you here, knowing I will miss some of you and feeling sorry for that already.

I wish I could name those of you at the school. I can't. I won't. But still, I offer my gratitude. Thank you to the administrators who trusted me, welcomed me to your school, and accommodated me in your schedule so I could be there every morning. Thank you and apologies to the administrative assistants who dealt with my contextual ignorance. Thank you to the teachers who generously shared your classrooms during your planning periods and patiently waited for me to pack up my recording equipment as your second period students came into your room. You could not have been kinder. There were other teachers around the school who just made me feel welcome by making space for me to interview students, inviting me to lunch, talking to me at extracurricular events, asking me about my project, telling me about their classes, and connecting about shared students. Thank you for making me feel like a part of the school. Of course, I will never be able to convey my gratitude adequately to the students who chose to take the classes we shared, who showed up, day after day, early morning after early morning, as seniors (mostly), even during spring break (I'm talking to that spring 2015 group here). I mean you showed up in all of the ways, all of you, and I count myself lucky. Lucky to have gotten to share the time and space with you, to have had the chance to get to know you, to have taught you and to have learned from you. Lucky, lucky me. Truly. Thank you. I offer unique gratitude to those of you who have stayed in touch and even read drafts of this work, particularly those I call Khalil, Mac, Parker, and Simon. Your insights continue to amaze me.

Thank you, Rebecca Colesworthy, my editor at SUNY Press, and the anonymous reviewers, for seeing the value in this project and challenging and supporting me as I worked to make it come to the fore.

Thank you for the initial institutional support from the National Council of Teachers of English (NCTE), the Spencer Foundation, the Ohio State University (OSU), and the University of Colorado Boulder (CU Boulder). With respect to NCTE, the funding through the Conference on English Education (CEE), before it was English Language Arts Teacher Educators (ELATE), was the first material support I received for this project. I will always appreciate Louann Reid coming up to me and saying, "It really is a good project." I needed those words. This grant was, truly, a seed grant. The Spencer Foundation then offered financial support through the bulk of data collection with a Small Research Grant, which felt big to me in so many ways. Finally, OSU provided faculty leave and CU Boulder provided a "room of one's own" with a view of the Flatirons so I could have the time and space to analyze the data and write this book into being. For all of this institutional support, I am genuinely grateful.

There also were people who made sure that that room of my own was not too lonely during the semester I spent in Boulder. Thank you, Kathy Schultz, for bringing me there, sharing meals with me, and welcoming me into your home. Thank you, Millie Gort, for being a model hostess, friend, and mom. Thank you, Sara Staley, for showing me a whole new way of being in the classroom. Thank you, Bethy Leonardi, for pizza, beer, data enthusiasm, and letting me know that the arm-wrestling scene needed to go in the book somewhere. Thank you, Elizabeth Dutro, for sharing with me the breakfast spot you used to go to with your kids and thinking this book might be something someday. Thank you, Wendy Glenn, for getting me to a coffee shop quickly so I could keep going back across the semester. Many data were analyzed in that coffee shop. Thank you, Arturo Cortez and José Ramón Lizárraga, for a delightful lunch, for driving Mindi and me to Wendy's (the colleague, not the fast-food chain), and for laughing so hard with us at our wailing child.

There are also the scholar friends at home who helped me think and feel my way through this project across years. Ryan Schey, thank you for being there every day of the first semester and organizing the data of every day of that semester and the following two semesters. You were always deeply invested in this project, as evidenced by how you felt my pain when the recorder failed, or, more likely, its user failed at recording.

I will always be grateful for your role in this project and for you, more broadly. Dave Bloome, I was taking your Discourse Analysis class while I was analyzing the data for this project, and echoes of your wisdom are throughout the whole; and Michiko, you are the one who got me there, week after week, via Skype, only a few short months before we were all Zooming everywhere. Thank you both. Shannon Winnubst, thank you for thinking I might be onto something by paying attention to the idea of movement. Thank you, Brian Edmiston and Pat Enciso, for gently helping me let go of my weak title and replacing it with a stronger one. (Titles really are hard for me.) Lauren Kenney, Mindi Rhoades, and Noah Demland read an early draft of the whole; that is such hard work that I desperately needed done. Thank you so much for taking that on. I could not be more grateful.

In addition to the scholarly work, there was the familial work. While I was off working on this book, there were people making sure things ran smoothly—well, smooth enough. Mostly, my partner, Mindi. Thank you, Mindi, for allowing me the time and space, in the early mornings when I taught the class and in the semester I spent in Boulder analyzing data. I know that was challenging, and I am grateful for your having accepted the challenge with such grace. I love that, and so much more, about you. Michiko Hikida, Francis Troyan, and the climbing parents also stepped up by hanging with and transporting my kids when I could not, and I am grateful to all of you. And I know it was not easy on you, Blais and Dottie Grey. Thank you for taking one for the team on this one. I'll try to do the same for you when it matters the most to you, over and over again. I love you with all my heart.

Introduction

Theoretical, Empirical, and Contextual

It was the middle of March 2015 in an LGBTQ+-themed literature course at a grassroots charter high school in a midsize city in the Midwestern region of the United States. It was first period, and the students were juniors and seniors—mostly seniors, so one might expect the energy to be low. I was teaching. We were shifting from one novel, *Aristotle and Dante Discover the Secrets of the Universe* (Sáenz, 2012), to another, *Brooklyn, Burning* (Brezenoff, 2011). *Aristotle and Dante* follows two Mexican American teenage boys through the end of their high school career in El Paso, Texas, in the late eighties as they come to understand themselves both individually and in relation to and in relationship with each other. *Brooklyn, Burning* describes a transient teen community and focuses on one teenager's love, loss, and love again, with a deliberate and consistent evasion of gender markers. Both books were, by spring break, read aloud in class in readers' theater style, where each student read either a narrator's part or a character's part throughout the reading. For the earlier book, *Aristotle and Dante*, I really had to pull students to volunteer to read parts, but that was not the case this time, with *Brooklyn, Burning*.

This time, I had multiple volunteers for multiple roles. One was for Fish, a local bar owner and a matriarch for transient queer youth. Darby and Sherry both wanted this role, so I said, "y'all rock-paper-scissors. Best of three." They were sitting on opposite sides of the square in which we had our desks. Sherry stood up first, then Darby stood up and walked over to Sherry. All students were engaged. They were watching. Darby and Sherry began, "One, two, three, shoot. One, two, three, shoot." I said, "Okay, so you're even. This is a tiebreaker." "One, two, three, shoot." Sherry

1

won. Darby walked back to her seat. I moved to the next role. Multiple students were interested. The class got quiet, watching me. Darby put her head down on her arms folded on her desk, but her face was up, looking at me, until Sherry said her name.

Sherry said, "You can be Fish. I'll be Scout."

Darby replied, "Are you sure?" Her voice sounded shaky.

Sherry nodded. "Yeah, you wanted Fish. You can be Fish."

Darby's voice was undeniably quivering. "Thank you."

The class as a whole seemed to sigh with relief as some students laughed, others chatted, and gazes moved around, from me to one another. Someone commented on how much Darby wanted to read the role of Fish; Sherry said, "I felt that. I saw the look on her face, and I felt that." Darby whispered to Sherry across the room, "I'll bring you coffee tomorrow."

I moved to the next role, asking who wanted to read one of the narrators. Three students wanted the role, including Parker and Rhys. They were sitting next to each other, so I told them to "rock-paper-scissors." Parker said, "Can't we just arm wrestle?" Rhys said, "Yeah, let's do that." And they both slammed their elbows on their desks and clutched each other's hand. Several students leaned in to get a better look. One student's jaw dropped. Another student said, "We are arm wrestling now?" She sounded almost appalled. Cobalt, the one whose jaw was dropped, jumped up and ran over to referee. Parker won.

Up until this point, the students competing for roles were queer identifying in various ways. In the next two rounds, however, people who had claimed queer identities and those who had embodied straight ones were competing against one another. In each of these cases, students moved together from across the room. Jokes were made about arm wrestling, but they were friendly, even warm. The students played rock-paper-scissors to determine readers. The final round went past the bell, but no one moved to leave until the round was over; only then did students gather their things to depart for their second-period classes.

In this brief classroom encounter, I saw students using their reading about diverse, LGBTQ+-themed literature to move closer to one another, both physically and interpersonally. I saw queer students moving closer to one another, as Sherry gave Darby the role she wanted most and as Parker and Rhys clutched hands to arm wrestle. But I also saw straight and cisgender students moving closer to queer ones, as Cobalt jumped up to referee the arm wrestling and pairs of students faced off to get the parts they wanted to read. There was competition, no doubt, but there was also so much laughter, even joy. There was agility. Importantly, there was also respect, as evidenced by students waiting until the last game was complete before packing up their things and leaving their seats. I understood this as an ethical classroom encounter.

This book argues that high school students in this course used language and literacy to move ideologically across differences in classroom encounters. By using language and literacy, I mean that students read, discussed, and wrote about LGBTQ+-themed literature as well as their lives more broadly. By moving across differences, I mean that they listened to one another—not all of the time, but sometimes, and when they did, they learned from one another, about one another as well as about themselves. They did not necessarily argue with and persuade one another. Indeed, sometimes they actively rejected one another, and sometimes with very good reason. But they moved. As they did so, the classroom became not a site of mere celebration of differences but rather a site of engaged negotiation and even struggle.

To make this argument, I engage with the work of Sara Ahmed and other queer scholars, some but not all of whom work in the realm of literacy education. Then I contextualize the study in pertinent empirical literature before contextualizing it socially and culturally in both broad terms and those specific to the particular school and classroom. I conclude this introduction by laying out the structure of the remainder of the book.

(Ethical) Encounters

Saying the opening vignette represents an ethical encounter raises the question of what an ethical encounter is. I start by exploring the notion of encounter before reflecting on what makes an encounter ethical. Ahmed (2000) defines an encounter as a face-to-face meeting that is "mediated" (p. 7)—in the case of a classroom, by a teacher and students—and in which there is an "asymmetry of power" (p. 8), which in this case exists between a teacher and students but also among students.

Encounters cannot be understood in isolation from the histories of those who constitute them. Consider classroom encounters in the United States, where there are pronounced histories of heteronormativity, homophobia, transphobia, sexism, racism, and the fallacy of white supremacy, among other sorts of oppression. We see this in classrooms where sex education ignores same-sex desires, where students are organized by gender, and where curricula center white men who are cisgender, heterosexual, and Christian. We also see it when teachers insist that students use English, and, more specifically, a "standard" English, demanding that students conceal or erase their home languages or dialects. Ahmed (2000) says, "The face to face of [any particular] encounter cannot . . . be detached or isolated from such broader relations of antagonism" (p. 9). Encounters, she asserts, "always hesitate between the domain of the particular—the face to face of this encounter—and the general—the framing of the encounter by broader relationships of power and antagonism. The particular encounter hence always carries *traces* of those broader relationships" (Ahmed, 2000, p. 8). If we think about this in terms of classrooms, this means that a white woman teaching *To Kill a Mockingbird* to Black students, for example, must acknowledge that she is implicated in the white-savior narrative on which the novel relies. For her to put Atticus Finch, a white lawyer, on a pedestal for trying the case in which Tom Robinson, a Black man falsely accused of rape, is acquitted reveals at least the potential of her seeing herself as one who saves Black students. The teacher positioning herself as a white savior, whether consciously or not, is destined to provoke the righteous anger in at least some of her Black students. Here we see the particular encounter between a teacher and students influenced by "broader relationships of power and antagonism," not only in the past, as represented by the novel, but also in the present, by contemporary dynamics in and beyond school.

Not only do encounters hover between the past and present, they also have implications for the future. In their exploration of Ahmed's encounters, Buys and Marotta (2021) explain, "Historical relations are made up of racialised, gendered, sexualised, and classed encounters and these impact present and, more importantly, future encounters" (p. 103). Indeed, Ahmed (2000) focuses on these future encounters when she asks "not only what made this encounter possible (its historicity), but also what does it make possible, what futures might it open up?" (p. 145). What kinds of futures an encounter might "open up" depends largely on the nature of the encounter. According to Buys and Marotta (2021), "Ahmed's notion of generous encounters illustrates how relations are not undifferentiated; some relations of proximity are healthier than others" (p. 110). Unethical encounters "can make some of us feel 'out of place' or not 'at home' where we are brought up" (Ahmed, 2021, p. 8). They can "objectify and marginalise" (Buys & Marotta, 2021, p. 108); they can "appropriat[e]" and "negate" (p. 109); they can "categorise" and "constrain" (p. 109). You can see how a white teacher teaching *To Kill a Mockingbird* to Black students may make students feel out of place in school, which they are required to attend. That said, healthier relations are possible; Ahmed calls these "ethical encounters."

An ethical encounter is where people come together, in moments in time, recognizing the "debts that are already accrued" (Ahmed, 2000, p. 154), talking across differences, and forming collectives "through the *very work that we need to do* in order to get closer to others" (p. 180). Ahmed (2000) argues that "a politics of encountering gets closer in order to allow the differences between us . . . to make a difference to the very encounter itself. The differences between us necessitate the dialogue, rather than disallow it—a dialogue must take place, precisely *because* we don't speak the same language" (p. 180). When Ahmed talks about dialogue, she is not, as I understand her, talking about what Bryson and de Castell (1993) call "some kind of pluralistic exhortation [to] 'dialogue across differences' " (p. 301). Instead, she means something more like how Aukerman (2021) uses the word: an unorderly exchange of ideas, a "struggle, as students thought with and against each other's possible meanings" (p. 9), "productive struggles over meaning" (p. 10). The differences she references may be defined by sexuality, gender, race, and religion, as well as those defined by families and many other ideological, social, and cultural constructs.[1] In a classroom, this sense of dialogue might mean a teacher naming problematic power dynamics and inviting students to discuss them. Consider a teacher reading *Roll of Thunder, Hear My Cry* (1976) with their students. Together, they might discuss why the N-word is used by the Black author, Mildred D. Taylor, in her representation of the Logans, an African American family living in the rural South in the

---

1. I will sometimes use the language of identities to refer to these constructs, and when I do, I am talking about identities as multiple and variable; I am talking about identities and the systems that constitute them as interlocking (see the 1977 Combahee River Collective Statement in BlackPast, 2012), intersectional (Hill Collins, 2019; Crenshaw, 1991), and mutually constitutive (Winnubst, 2006).

1930s. The teacher might also explain that they are going to use the term "the N-word" instead of reading it verbatim during their read-alouds and invite students to discuss this decision. Everyone might not agree on Taylor's decision to use the word or the teacher's decision not to, but engaging in the dialogue across differences is a conversation that matters beyond the reading of the book.

Alexander (2008) asserts that "our differences—often systematically defined and constructed along lines of race, ethnicity, gender, and class—impact our ability to speak for ourselves, tell our truths, and make common cause with others" (p. 8). In other words, our differences impact our ability to communicate and connect. Therefore, I look not only at the that which hinders our ability to communicate and connect but also at the moments in which we overcome those obstacles and do it anyway. Encounters across differences, thus, are "bound up with responsibility" (Ahmed, 2000, p. 180). Those involved must "thin[k] about how we might work with, and speak to, others, or how we might inhabit the world *with* others" (Ahmed, 2000, p. 180). According to Ahmed, this requires "the 'painstaking labour' of getting closer, of speaking to each other, and of working *for* each other," which results in getting "closer to 'other others' " (Ahmed, 2000, p. 180). It is through such "acts of alignment" that "we can reshape the very bodily form of the community, as a community that is yet to come" (Ahmed, 2000, p. 180). It is not always and everywhere appropriate to do this work. Indeed, Ahmed (2000) states that "we need to pay attention to the *shifting conditions* in which encounters between others, and between other others, take place" (p. 19). It is only by paying attention to encounters that we can begin to answer Ahmed's (2000) question: "How can we encounter an other in such a way, in a *better* way, that allows something to give?" (p. 154).

Thus, in an ethical encounter people listen to one another; they notice what moves them and what fails to move them (Ahmed, 2000). Such listening and noticing requires a degree of proximity, but Ahmed (2000) quotes Iris Marion Young in pointing out that those who have been othered, or minoritized and oppressed, " 'would prefer a stance of respectful distance, . . . and thus [others] must listen [to them] carefully across the distance' " (p. 156). In other words, in an ethical encounter, people must be close enough to listen but not so close as to threaten. How close one can be without being threatening depends on the shared histories and the trusted promises of futures. Ahmed (2000) states, "An ethical communication is about a certain way of holding proximity and distance together: one gets close enough to others to be touched by that which cannot be simply got across. In such an encounter, 'one' does not stay in place, or one does not stay safely at a distance (there is no space which is not implicated in the encounter). It is through getting closer, rather than remaining at a distance, that the impossibility of pure proximity can be put to work or made to work" (p. 157). An ethical encounter is characterized by one's "refusal to identify the other as enemy" and commitment to assume "intimate responsibility for the other" (Ahmed, 2000, p. 137). (When she uses the term "the other," Ahmed means people who have been othered, like those who have been minoritized, not just people who are other than you in one way or another, although that might also be the case.) Aukerman (2021) argues that "ethical" defines how "we should be in the world with each other" (p. 12). A teacher striving to foster ethical encounters in a classroom listens to students and notices when something invigorates them and when something deflates them, whether it is an assignment or an interaction with a peer. When a student comes into the class looking angry, the teacher checks in with them but does not pry, offers support or alternatives but does not demand an explanation. The teacher positions themself as an advocate for students in myriad ways. They never "stay in place" but move in response to and with respect for students. Ethical encounters, then, require movement both toward and within encounters.

Moving toward Encounters

We only encounter one another when we move, from one place to another. When we move, there is always, out there, the idea of home, where, in Ahmed's (2000) words, "one has already been enveloped, inhabited by" (p. 90). Home is often "*sentimentalised* as a space of belonging" (Ahmed, 2000, p. 89), but home is more complicated than that. Consider, for example, the home of a child who comes to understand themself as something other than straight or cisgender. The child may be ostracized by other family members, in their shared home. Indeed, "if we think of 'home' purely as proximity and familiarity, then we fail to recognise the relationships of estrangement and distance within the home" (Ahmed, 2000, p. 139). A home does not mean the absence of strangers, if we rely on Ahmed's understanding of the stranger: "strangers are under scrutiny by those who consider themselves at home or in place" (Ahmed, 2021, p. 19). Ahmed (2021) offers, as an example, how "people of colour in white organisations are treated as guests, temporary residents in someone else's home" (p. 17). That is to say, they, like some queer youth, are made to feel as strangers in their own homes. Minoritized people need ideological homes where people are "like-minded and understand the danger and the price of such work to sustain themselves" (Gonçalves, 2005, p. 15), where people can "work steadily toward understanding [their] own values and the values of others" (p. 13). One can have many ideological homes (Gonçalves, 2005), and the boundaries between them and not-home are, according to Ahmed (2000), permeable.

When someone moves away from one person or community, where they move toward depends on what is in their ideological line of vision, according to Ahmed. One cannot move toward a trans community, for example, when they think they are the only one experiencing gender in ways beyond cisnormativity. They must know that other transgender people exist in the world in order to move toward them, and such movement is of immense consequence, and not just for the one moving. When one moves toward a person or community, that person or those people in the community are "touched by what comes near" (Ahmed, 2010, p. 22). People come to understand themselves and one another, and, in doing so, they influence one another (Ahmed, 2000). According to Ahmed (2000), people are thus "perpetually reconstituted" through encounters (p. 7). Relatedly, encounters that result from movement between and among people and communities broaden people's understanding of the world and the people in it. Waite (2017) reflects on such encounters as "the moment we come into contact with what challenges, affirms, resists, or does not fit in with our prior knowledge of ourselves or others" (p. 134). Waite (2017) argues that "without this movement, this revision of understanding, we would be left with [a] kind of reduction and simplification" (p. 143). Waite (2017) asserts that "to move toward multiplicity is to live in a world with more possibility," which, Waite reminds us, quoting Judith Butler, " 'is not a luxury; it is as crucial as bread' " (p. 153). That is to say, broadening understanding matters.

Gonçalves (2005) found that students who had more narrow and static understandings of themselves and others saw "differences as impossible obstacles" or "ignore[ed] differences altogether" (p. 12). Either way, according to Gonçalves (2005), "leaves in place the customs, norms, and laws that stigmatize" (p. 12). In contrast, when speakers "claim[ed] and name[d] their own multiple, in-flux identities, they [we]re more likely to see all people . . . as complicated and in process rather than as a static enemy image. Likewise, when speakers acknowledge[d] their own multiple and in-process identities, audience members [we]re more likely to see [people] as in-process and complicated rather than as a static pariah image" (Gonçalves, 2005, pp. 12–13). By seeing themselves and others as multiple and variable, they came to understand differences "as a source of new perspectives" and thus understand others as potential allies, to whom they could speak more easily (Gonçalves, 2005, p. 13). Thus, as Ahmed (2000) asserts, encounters shape worlds (p. 8). Without movement toward encounters, movement within encounters becomes impossible.

MOVING WITHIN ENCOUNTERS

In an effort to explore the notion of movement within an encounter, Ahmed (2000) reflects on encountering a text. She writes about the many tensions in the experience but also how the "narrative moves [her] forward" (p. 159) and how, in her words, "I touch the pages. I am moved. Something gives" (p. 154). This is not physical movement, necessarily, but ideological.

Waite (2017) uses water as a metaphor for understanding ideological movement between and among people and communities. Waite (2017) talks about "becoming liquid" when discussing "ways of moving students, or helping them to move themselves, away from dualistic constructions of body, of argument, and of categorical placement" (p. 25). Waite (2017) tries to understand "what it means to *become water*, moving water, which, in the end, resists its own freezing up" (p. 25). The alternative, Waite (2017) asserts, is "to become stone, to become the reader who cannot be moved or repositioned" (p. 164). I am not just talking about readers, however; I am talking about people who read among those who engage in many other forms of communication. In doing so, people may either become rigid in their thinking and cold in their feeling or, alternatively, become fluid. Becoming fluid does not mean simply taking the ideological shape of those read or heard. Indeed, Waite reminds us that water cuts canyons. But Waite (2017) also considers turning into liquid like "dissolving" (p. 134), like sugar dissolves in coffee or tea. Waite (2017) contends that dissolving "always involves movement—the kind of movement solids are not capable of" (p. 134). So, when one's ideas dissolve, they "never, ultimately, disappear, but when they become liquid and fluid as opposed to solid, it makes them movable; it makes them open to evaporation" (Waite, 2017, p. 135). The metaphor is not scientifically perfect, but no metaphor is perfect, by definition. Still, the idea of becoming ideologically water or liquid so that one can read, listen, and learn—so that one can also write, speak, and teach—so that one can *move* among people and communities is one that I find useful.

Moving among people and communities, however, is not an independent endeavor. Ahmed (2000) talks about being "moved by the other" (p. 156). This raises a question of agency, a question underscored by Gonçalves (2005) and Waite (2017), who study how students learn to move their audiences, whether those are students on a speakers' bureau talking to their audiences in an effort to move them or writing students striving to move the readers of their writing. Waite also talks about teachers moving students, although this is not Waite's focus. Thus, in these ways and others, people move themselves and others. Ahmed (2021) further points out that one can even be *re*moved by another. But no one moves in isolation from others.

To be moved by an other, though, depends on listening, listening that Aukerman (2021) describes as "rare, real listening to understand" rather than to instruct (p. 8), a "careful[ly] sustained listening, [a] willingness to consider multiple perspectives, [a] deliberate building upon what others have to say even in the presence of passionate disagreement" (p. 12). Further, movement depends on emotions. Emotions, as social and cultural practices, can provoke ideological movement. Ahmed (2014) describes emotions as "*doing things*" (p. 209). She says they "involve different movements towards and away from others" (Ahmed, 2014, p. 209). She says they are "relational: they involve (re)actions of relations of 'towardness' or 'awayness' in relation to such objects" (Ahmed, 2014, p. 8). Here, "objects" may be people and communities. Whether emotions provoke movement toward or away depends on the emotion. Ahmed (2014) tells us, "Different emotions . . . involve different orientations toward objects and others" (p. 210). Fear, disgust, and shame, she argues, can conjure repulsion, or provoke movement away from. Love can conjure attraction, or provoke movement toward. But it's not that simple: "the intensification [of emotions such as fear, hate, disgust, or pain can] involv[e] moving away from the body of the other, or moving towards that body in an act of violence, and then moving away" (Ahmed, 2014, p. 194). In other words, movement within encounters does not ensure ethical encounters, but it does allow for the possibility. Indeed, encounters are where Ahmed (2000) sees possibility, the "possibility of something giving—not me or you—but something giving in the very encounter between a 'me' and a 'you'" (p. 154). This notion of "giving" is central to the idea of ethical encounters.

So, there is movement toward encounters and movement in encounters, and both depend on agility. The movement may be dramatic but is more likely to be subtle, more like giving. Ethical encounters depend on movement toward and in encounters. It is not that all encounters surrounded by and comprising movement are ethical; they are not. And a person can be ethical while taking a firm stance. But in order for an encounter to happen, there must be movement toward it, and in order for an encounter to be ethical, there must be give among those in it.

LGBTQ+-Themed Literature in Secondary Classrooms

This book portrays, explores, and examines a study of a secondary English language arts course with a particular focus on LGBTQ+-themed literature. Such courses have been the sites of the majority of studies of LGBTQ+-inclusive curricula (e.g., Athanases, 1996; Blazar, 2009; Carey-Webb, 2001; Cruz, 2013; Greenbaum, 1994; Hoffman, 1993; Reese, 1998; Schey & Uppstrom, 2010; Vetter, 2010). Reviews of these studies (Blackburn & Schey, 2017; Clark & Blackburn, 2009) and others in middle and elementary classrooms (Atkinson & DePalma, 2009; Epstein, 2000; Gonzales, 2010; Hamilton, 1998; Moita-Lopes, 2006; Ryan & Hermann-Wilmarth, 2018; Schall & Kauffmann, 2003; Simon et al., 2018) show that they were conducted in heterosexist if not homophobic contexts (Blackburn & Schey, 2017; Clark & Blackburn, 2009). In turn, students in the classes are positioned as straight and often homophobic (Blackburn & Clark, 2011; Blackburn & Schey, 2017; Clark & Blackburn, 2009). While some studies have engaged LGBTQ+ adolescents and young adults with LGBTQ+-themed literature in queer-friendly contexts (Blackburn, 2002/2003, 2003a, 2003b, 2005a, 2005b; de Castell & Jenson, 2007; Halverson, 2007) and a few have studied the selection, reading, and discussion of LGBTQ+-themed literature with LGBTQ+ and ally youth in queer-friendly contexts (Blackburn & Clark, 2011; Blackburn et al., 2015), none of these queer-friendly contexts were classrooms or schools. Notable exceptions, beyond this project, are Helmer's (2015, 2016a, 2016b) dissertation study of a high school gay and lesbian literature course and Kenney's (2010) chapter about being an out high school English teacher.

In most studies of classroom and school contexts, however, students were assumed to be straight and/or homophobic, and they engaged with LGBTQ+-themed literature in isolated classrooms and singular lessons or units. Typically, adults chose texts for didactic purposes, to expose students to issues pertinent to LGBTQ+ people (Blackburn & Clark, 2011). This meant the texts worked as windows into the lives of LGBTQ+ people but not as mirrors of LGBTQ+ people (Sims, 1982). Moreover, texts selected were almost entirely what Cart and Jenkins (2006) categorize as homosexual visibility (HV) rather than gay assimilation (GA) or queer community or consciousness (QC). This means that the chosen texts made LGBTQ+ people visible, but they did not show that LGBTQ+ people are like straight people, as GA literature would, or represent LGBTQ+ people in supportive communities, as QC literature would. Even though some version of the acronym *LGBTQ+* is used in many of these studies, they mostly focus on the inclusion of lesbian- and/or gay-themed literature and not bisexual- or trans-themed literature.

This book strives to fill in gaps in the field by presenting a study conducted in a classroom and school that actively worked to be queer-friendly, where it was estimated that 30 percent of the student population identified as LGBTQ+, and where it was expected and enforced that students were not homophobic or transphobic. These expectations were evident in the policy and practices of the school, teachers, and administration. For example, many students talked about being told, when they toured the school to determine whether it was good match, that there was no tolerance for homophobia or transphobia in the school and if that was a problem for them they should consider a different option for high school. Texts that promote LGBTQ+ visibility as well as agency were read across a semester. They were used as windows, mirrors, and doors into others' worlds (Botelho & Rudman, 2009; Sims Bishop, 1990). As a result, this book provides new insights on the possibilities for engaging adolescents with LGBTQ+-themed literature in classrooms and schools.

That said, the argument I make is not one about simply including LGBTQ+-themed literature. Inclusion alone is too simple of a solution to too complex of a problem. Kumashiro (2001) identifies two reasons that curricular inclusion cannot solve the problem of discrimination in classrooms and schools: "First, countless differences exist in society (such as differences based on race, class, gender, sexuality, religion, [dis]ability, language, body size, and the intersections of these differences), making it literally impossible to be fully 'inclusive.' Second, even if all differences could be named and included, the very act of naming and including difference could operate in contradictory ways" (p. 5). Even if a class only read biographies of one another all semester or even all year long, the curriculum would still only be partial. Not only would it exclude people in the world who are not in the class, but biographies always include some details and exclude others, by necessity; they are always located in some time or place, or some times and places, but not all of them, and decidedly not the ones in the present. Inclusion is quite simply beyond reach.

My contribution, rather, is about movement. Unlike the impossibility of full inclusion, moving among one another in classroom encounters is not only possible, it is all but inevitable. I show how students move closer to and farther away from one another through discussing literature and lives and how this sometimes invites students to move in and connect rather than stand back and dismiss or decipher. Such movement does not require that people relinquish their values. Encountering other people, values, and communities may even strengthen our own. But movement prevents stagnation. It interrupts the ossification of values; it discourages rigidity and encourages imagination in relationships.

Studying classroom encounters in this way can show teachers that they can expect and even demand such movement of students, since students do it all the time; really, people do it all the time. Such examinations can show researchers another way to understand people and their communities as dramatically dynamic. Some of the encounters I examine here were miserable for some people. Some of them were quite joyful. We, as members of the classroom community, needed the latter to endure the former, but we, as members of much larger communities, need the former to make change. Those miserable encounters can reveal what needs to be changed, and they can be a catalyst for that change. More broadly speaking, we need to be able to talk across differences, to understand one another better; we need to be able to be together and apart with more compassion and respect even if not more comfort; we need to be able, in Ahmed's words, to give.

Contextualizing with Breadth and Depth

To contextualize the project, I first talk about the broader social and cultural context. I then describe the school and class as well as the students and teacher in the class. Thus, I provide both breadth and depth in my contextualization of the study. The study itself was a blend of ethnography

(Blommaert & Dong, 2020; Heath & Street, 2008) and teacher research (Cochran-Smith & Lytle, 1993, 2009).[2] The book focuses on classroom encounters from the aforementioned LGBTQ+-themed literature course, which I taught three consecutive semesters between January of 2015 and June of 2016.[3] In the three classes, students navigated their relationships with sexual, gender, and racial identities as well as with religion and family. While these identities are always important in the United States, their importance was emphasized at the time of these classes. Race was underscored during this time because the Black Lives Matter movement had grown in power and prominence since its inception in 2013, particularly in the 2014 protests in Ferguson, Missouri, in response to the murder of Michael Brown by a police officer. Moreover, Black Lives Matter was playing an active role in campaigns for the 2016 US presidential election, which was just getting started. Donald J. Trump's campaign to be the Republican nominee for the presidential election relied heavily on racist and more broadly xenophobic values but also on deeply conservative Christian values. I am not saying that these necessarily overlap, but where they did was at the heart of his campaign. As a result, not only was race a foregrounded discussion, so too was religion. Families, primarily parents, became central to my analysis because students talked about their families so often throughout classroom encounters. Although many of the readings provoked such discussions, it was not a topic I deliberately raised. It was one the students just kept returning to. It was important to them and therefore important to me.

THE SCHOOL

The school was located just inside the perimeter of a midsize Midwestern city, in a two-story, dark-glass building that was once office space. Although the school was housed on the first floor, the large sign with the

---

2. I discuss the methods in more detail in the appendix of this book.

3. During the first semester, I was accompanied by Ryan Schey, who is now a friend and colleague but was, at the time, a doctoral student working as a research apprentice in the class. We both attended the class daily; I was primarily in charge of teaching the class, and he was primarily in charge of gathering and organizing data. (To read more about our work together on this project, see Blackburn & Schey, 2018; Schey & Blackburn, 2019a, 2019b.) In the second and third semesters, I assumed responsibility for data collection, but Ryan, by this time a graduate research associate on the project, continued organizing the data.

school's name in block lettering on colorful squares was on the exterior of the second floor of the building. It was surrounded by a sidewalk and a parking lot, with another, smaller version of the sign on a placard in front of the building. The entrance was discreet, with the school's name, address, and hours in small white letters alongside the two glass doors in the center of the building. When I entered through those doors, I walked past a counter where administrative assistants welcomed students into the building. Behind them were the offices of administrators. Just past the counter was the main corridor of the high school, which extended right toward the science, music, and dance classrooms and left toward English, math, and theater classrooms, among others. For the classrooms where I taught, I turned left. I describe those rooms in detail later in this section.

The school was an arts-based, grassroots, charter high school. Included in its mission, vision, and articulated beliefs were words like *safe*, *inclusive*, *progressive*, *accepting*, and *respectful*. Its nondiscrimination policy used enumerated language including "race, ethnicity, country of origin, gender, sexual orientation, gender identity, disability, veteran status, religion, class, [and] age." LGBTQ+ students were actively recruited to the school at events such as local Pride parades and screenings of films pertinent to LGBTQ+ people. School personnel and policies communicated to the students an expectation that they not be homophobic or transphobic, contributing to a queer-friendly environment.

Students who attended this school mostly elected to join it. As a charter school, it was no one's neighborhood school. In my initial interviews with students, when I asked the story of how they came to this school, I learned that they were mostly seeking an arts-based experience, a queer-friendly context, or an alternative to their home schools. According to some students in a class discussion, parents understood the school as "the gay school." But it was not only the gay school. According to its policies, "it thrive[d] on the diversity of its members." When I asked students, in interviews, to describe the school, Desiree, a Black, cis, straight young woman, said,

> It's, well, you have to be able not to judge, and like when situations come up you have to be able to know how to handle it. Like I've learned that, since the course of being here, I've learned how to handle different situations different ways, because I used to be really hotheaded, and it's a really accepting school, and it's not—you won't find any other school like

it. . . . I can be myself here, and that's taught, like, it's taught me how to, like, love myself and learn and, like, develop into the person I am today, because I don't think I could have done that four years ago.

Similarly, in another interview, Jenna, who is also a Black, cis, straight young woman, said, "If you're looking to get an education and not, like, be bullied in the process of it, and be comfortable with, like, who you are, you should definitely come here." Jenna always interviewed with Khalil, a cis, gay young man who sometimes identified as Black and other times as multiracial, which I discuss further in chapter 3. In this same interview, to the same question about how they would "describe [the school] to someone who has never been here before," he said, "I always tell them the education and the non-bullying and the arts. . . . I'm like, if you want that anchor education at the same time, [this school is], like, the perfect place to be."

Of course, not all students experienced it that way. Delilah, a cis, straight Latina, experienced the antibullying aspect of the school differently. She explained, "The majority group that come here are, like, all bullied, or something's like, you know, wrong. And there's this other crowd that's like, 'What? No, we just wanted to escape our home school.'" She counted herself among the latter group and said, "We don't really know how to, like, encounter things. . . . Because we don't want to push anybody's buttons, but we also don't want to, like, make someone cry, because people are really oversensitive. . . . [So] the people who come here to escape their home schools just stay in their own little circle." I followed up by asking if these two groups were racially identifiable. "No, it's a mixture," she responded. "The ones that are, like, bullied are more Caucasian . . . or, like, Asian-ish. The ones that are not, that just escaped [their home schools], are either Hispanic or Black or, like, white, or, like, just in general just more diverse." So, while students elected to come to the school, they had different reasons. One of my students even explained that he came to this school after being expelled from his previous school. While students being given a second chance at this school was not unheard of, it was atypical. And though some experienced it as "the perfect place to be," others experienced as a little more complicated than that.

Among the little over three hundred students enrolled at the school during the time of this study, administrators at the school estimated that 30 percent identified as LGBTQ+. In terms of race and ethnicity, 56 percent of students were white, 26 percent were African American, 10 percent were multiracial, 6 percent were Latina/o, 1 percent were Asian, and 1 percent were Pacific Islander. (Here, I am using the school's terminology.)

The Class

Over the three semesters, the class met in two different rooms of teachers who had first-period study hall. During the first semester, the class met in another English teacher's room. When I walked in the door, I walked into a large, rectangular room. The wall opposite the door had windows all the way across it. The wall immediately to the right and directly across from the windows was painted a vibrant green. These two were the shorter two of the walls. On the green wall there were two bookshelves and some cabinets, and the host teacher invited me to store our class books on one of the shelves, which I did. The wall to the left as I entered was the back wall. Opposite, the front wall held a clock, a whiteboard, a smart board, and a podium, as well as a collection of inspirational posters. The teacher's desk was along the front wall in the corner diagonally opposite the door. In between were twelve light-gray tables with two burgundy chairs at each. While they were typically in three horizontal rows of four tables each, facing the front of the room, I moved six of the tables into a rectangle in front of the whiteboard, where I wrote the agenda each morning before class. Once we started recording the class, Ryan typically placed the video camera in the corner opposite both the teacher's desk and the door. At the end of every class, students would help Ryan and me reposition the tables and chairs so that they were like the host teacher wanted them for his second-period class.

During the second and third semesters, the class met in a math teacher's room. The room was small, windowless, and mostly gray. The wall with the door was one of the two long walls in the rectangular room. As I walked in the door, to the right there was a red-fabric shoe rack for students' phones and a small whiteboard on the wall. The teacher's desk was directly in front of me, along the back wall, and there was a floor lamp, a bookshelf, and a Minecraft poster behind the teacher's desk. There were some pieces of paper taped both to the wall to the right when I walked in and along the back wall. The papers to the right were schedules and reminders. The papers on the back wall were students' drawings. The front wall was almost entirely covered by a whiteboard and a smart board. There was also a screen that could be pulled down over the whiteboard for using the projector, attached to the ceiling. There was a small cabinet from which technological devices like a laptop or DVD player could be connected to the projector. The student desks were stand-alone and moveable, with navy-blue chairs, metal frames underneath for holding students' things, and light, wood-like desktops. Typically, they were organized in six vertical rows of four desks facing the whiteboards, but every morning before class I moved enough desks for the students in my small class into a circle. I typically sat at one of the desks closer to the whiteboard, where I always wrote the agenda for the day. Once I started recording the class, I placed a microphone in the center of the circle and a tripod with the video camera diagonally opposite from the teacher's desk. That's the corner where I stored my materials in two rolling carts under a table—one cart for books anyone could borrow and another for any other supplies, like lesson plans, tape, scissors, markers, and so on. At the end of every class, students would help me replace the desks so that they were like the host teacher wanted them for his second-period class. Both teachers were very kind about sharing their space with me, and I was and am so grateful for their hospitality.

The class itself, like most classes at the school, met four days per week, with the fourth weekly meeting being a double block of time. The curriculum each term was broken down into units (see the tables in the appendix.) In the first term, I started with a unit on nonfiction and moved to one on memoir, but at the end of that term a student asked me who James Baldwin was, and I felt absolutely deflated. The following two terms, I started with a unit I called History and Poetry. In those terms I combined the units on nonfiction and memoir. In all three terms I taught a unit on fiction, and in the first and third terms I taught one on short stories (we simply ran out of time in the second term).

I prioritized young adult literature, like the novels *Aristotle and Dante Discover the Secrets of the Universe* (Sáenz, 2012) and *Brooklyn, Burning* (Brezenhoff, 2011), both of which I describe above, and *If You Could Be Mine* (Farizan, 2013), which I describe briefly below. That said, I also included literature written for and marketed to adults, like excerpts from Alison Bechdel's (2006) *Fun Home*, Terry Galloway's (2009) *Mean Little Deaf Queer*, and Audre Lorde's (1982) *Zami*. I strove to bring texts that represented a broad range of experiences, with particular attention to sexuality and gender but also to race and ethnicity, as evidenced in the selection above, which includes representations of Mexican American, Iranian, and African American queer characters and authors, as well as those who live in poverty or with disabilities. The units reveal my commitment to exploring a wide range of genres—poetry, memoir, novels, short stories, and others—but I also worked to include a range of media, including photo essays, films, graphic narratives, songs, and videos. Students also responded to these texts in a variety of ways. In our History and Poetry unit and when we studied novels, students wrote collections of journal entries and read and responded to those of classmates. When we studied memoirs, short stories, and essays, students ultimately wrote versions of their own. In short, I wanted to invite students to explore LGBTQ+-themed literature in as many ways as I could imagine and manage.

Moreover, I was committed to creating an ethical classroom through pedagogy. This is not to say I always fulfilled this commitment. Indeed, when writing about her own ethical literacy-classroom practice, Gonçalves (2005) writes that ethical principles "are not easy to practice," sometimes "nearly impossible," but they are made more possible with "deep listening . . . humility and compassion" (p. 133). The principles they lay out include "self-reflection, separation of judgments from observations," "use of dialogue," and "a focus on making allies and common ground" (Gonçalves, 2005, p. 132). They suggest that teachers "foreground connection" (Gonçalves, 2005, p. 143), "meet students wherever they [are]" (p. 144), and "revisit situations" (p. 144). Although Gonçalves is focused on collegiate teaching rather than secondary teaching, their exploration of pedagogical ethics in literacy classrooms resonates with my own. This was evident in some the repeated phrases that I came to hear as refrains as I listened to the recordings of our class discussions, like "What do you think?" and "Let me tell you this story real quick." There were also pedagogical complements, like anticipating, attending, and debriefing after school dances and performances and other events, which bolstered the relationships among us, allowing them to endure more difficult interactions when necessary.

THE STUDENTS

Many who took the class were drawn to the content, but there were also logistical motivations, like needing a first-period class that filled an English requirement so they could leave school early for work and still graduate on time, as an example. Notable exceptions were two white, cis, straight young men who told me they were "put" in the class by an administrator as a "joke." Still, the expectation was that homophobia and transphobia would be worked against, as they were in the school. Indeed, when students referenced their own negative feelings about LGBTQ+ people, it was with typically with regret. For example, in a class discussion, Vic, a Black lesbian, said, "I remember when I was in seventh grade, like, um, well, like, I was kind of questioning my sexuality, but I was also a little bit homophobic, but like, I'm just, like, I'm not anymore, obviously, but, um, I used to feel that way." In other words, the class was a place where homophobia could be named but not really claimed.

Across the three semesters, thirty-two students took the class, and thirty-one were participants in the study. In the first class, there were fourteen students (thirteen participants); in the second class, there were eight students; and in the third, there were ten. In the classes, there was a lot of experimentation and fluidity in terms of sexual identities and gender identities and expression. I provide a loose sense of the classes in these terms here, but please forgive the innately problematic nature of the categories I offer below and then complicate throughout the book. Across the three semesters, with respect to sexuality, about half of the students identified as straight, about one-quarter of the students identified on the opposite end of the sexuality continuum, and the remaining one-quarter identified somewhere in between. "In between" here includes identities such as bisexual, pansexual, fluid, and questioning. In the first class, five out of thirteen participants identified as straight, three as gay, and five as somewhere in between. In the second class, three out of eight students identified as straight; three as gay, including one as homoromantic; and two as somewhere in between. And in the third class, eight students identified as straight and two as gay. With respect to gender, across all classes, six out of thirty-one participants identified as boys or men, including one who identified as a trans man. Nineteen identified as cisgender girls or women. The six remaining students were experimenting with gender, and they ranged in their gender expression anywhere from I saw no evidence of this experimentation to their experimentation being quite visible to me in their daily expressions of gender. Their self-identifications were multiple and variable.

Racial identities were generally more stable among these students. Among the thirty-one students, twenty-two identified as white and nine as people of color, including four people who identified as Black, two as biracial Asian and white, one as biracial Black and white, one as Latina, and one as multiracial. The first class was composed almost entirely of white people, with one person identifying as biracial Asian and white. The second class included five white people and three people of color, two of whom identified as Black and one as biracial Black and white. The third class included five white people and five people of color, two of whom identified as Black, one as Latina, one as multiracial, and one as biracial Asian and white. Throughout the book, I describe students with more precision when needed based on my understanding of them over time.

In more general terms, the class size was always small, ranging from eight to fourteen students. Queer kids constituted over half of the first and second classes. This was not the case in the third class, in which about a fifth of the students were queer. I suspect, but cannot know, that the first class was the largest because it included students who had been waiting for something like this to come along. It's the only class of mine that included juniors and seniors, and it seemed like it took some effort for juniors to work it into their schedules. Over the three terms, the class became increasingly racially diverse; all but one student identified as white in the first class, and about half of the students identified as white and half as people of color in the third class. I suspect, but again cannot know, that this was due to word getting around that despite the stereotype that being gay is a white-people issue, and despite the teacher being white, people of color were well represented in the course content. This came to my attention as students of color in the school but not in my class started coming by the room I used in the morning, before the first-period class, and borrowing books I recommended. One student wanted only poetry by Black lesbians and would regularly exchange one book for another. Several visibly Muslim students wanted *If You Could Be Mine* (Farizan, 2013), a novel exploring a lesbian relationship between teenage girls in Tehran, Iran, as the girls come to terms with their love and related political limitations. The students seemed to be talking about the book among one another. But these were students who were not in the class and therefore not in the study.

As such, it is worth paying attention to who was not in the study, too. Religion played a role, as I suggest above. There were students in the class who talked actively and critically about their Christian and Catholic families—typically separating the denominations using those terms—as homophobic and transphobic, but these students were still in the class. Muslim students, however, were not, even though they were a visible part of the student body. As I mention above, some Muslim students came by and borrowed books; one Muslim young man came by on the day students shared their memoirs, watched theirs, and performed his own improvised memoir. Then there was one student who was in the class for a bit before their parents withdrew them from the class and another student who was in the class for a full semester but whose parents did not consent to her participation in the study. I do not know whether religion was a point of contention or not, but the focus on LGBTQ+ people certainly was, as I learned from some of the students who were in the class and the study but had encountered some resistance to their participation from their parents. For example, Carter explained that her parents were reluctant to sign the study's consent form, and I offered to address any of their questions or concerns. Carter and I discussed the situation:

> CARTER: [My mom] had questions about the "purpose" part. I was like, I—like, the way that she was asking her question I didn't understand. . . . She had, she was like . . . she asked if uh, like, "What does that mean? When it says, like, ask you, like, how it affects students or whatever." I was like—oh, she was like, "What? To see if you're, like, gay at the end of year?" I was like—

> DR. BLACKBURN: No no no. [*laughs*] [indecipherable] I'm not trying to convert you.

> CARTER: I was like, "No." I'd already said—I was like, "Mom, no. What is wrong with you?" She was like, "I'm just asking." I was like, "No, just sign the paper."

> DR. B.: I love that your mom would ask that. That's great, because I would rather people ask that than think that, and just walk around with that thought. So, so yes. The idea is not to turn anyone gay. . . . No, this is good, this is good. So, I'm not trying to turn anyone gay for sure. What I am trying to do is that [for] people who identify as gay, to make them feel welcome in schools. And then for people who identify—who don't identify as gay to, uh, help them to dev—to identify as allies so that they can, like . . . lear[n] to be, uh, kind of [the] best friends and classmates of people, of LGBT people, that you can be. Uh, so that people do better, you know, so there's less of a suicide rate and less of, uh, failure rates in schools. . . . So please, please communicate to mom: I am not trying to convert anybody. That is not my game, I promise. And—

CARTER: Yeah, right, I was like, "Too late."

DR. B.: All right, I don't think, I don't think that kind of conversion is possible anyway. You don't get turned gay.

This conversation, though, and others like it, prompted me, in closing interviews, to ask whether the students experienced any challenges at home as a result of taking the class. Khalil said, "No. I think it made . . . life at home better . . . because my dad, he, he wasn't really understanding everything. He would ask a question, and I was like, 'Oh, I can answer that now.' . . . So it made life much easier . . . because I knew more about it, and, like, just reading other people's stories, I'm like, 'Okay.' " In other words, not all students who wanted to take the class could, for a variety of reasons, and for some students who managed to take the class, doing so took some maneuvering, but among those who did, at least Khalil found some advantage to having done so. And I had the privilege to teach and learn with them.

THE TEACHER-RESEARCHER

As I mention above, in the first semester, I was primarily a teacher and secondarily a researcher, and Ryan Schey was primarily a researcher and secondarily a teacher, but in the second and third terms I was fully a teacher-researcher. This was a role that I had practice in. I conducted my first teacher research project during my master's program under the guidance of JoBeth Allen. I conducted a practitioner inquiry project for my dissertation under the guidance of Susan Lytle. Moreover, I worked with Caroline Clark to guide teachers in their own teacher-research projects through a teacher inquiry group we initiated and facilitated with Jim Buckley and Jeane Copenhaver-Johnson. I was excited to be assuming the role of a teacher-researcher again.

It was different, though, coming from the university and teaching in a high school classroom. I was a bit of a novelty. A teacher and friend suggested that I go by Dr. Blackburn because students seemed excited to be taking a class with a college professor. This positioned me as having a certain kind of authority, but it also positioned me with a different sort of lack of authority in that I did not know and use the school practices and procedures like others did. This sort of tension, between having and lacking power, was evident in other traits I claimed. For example, being queer and cis positioned me as both experienced and inexperienced in the content of the course: LGBTQ+. Being white limited my understanding of the texts by and about people of color as well as of students of color. I had and continue to have to work hard to compensate for that limitation. Being middle-aged limited my understanding of the young people with whom I worked. I had been young once, but I wasn't when I was teaching this class, so I needed to listen carefully to the young people with whom I spent time in order to come closer to understanding what they were experiencing.

Thus, my identities shaped my positionality, which influenced, and often limited, my teaching but also my research. Miller (2020) offers guidance on negotiating such dynamics: "the key to leaning into this work is to open up space for people to be who they are and to respond with gentleness, kindness, and respect, and to have patience with, and compassion for, one's self and the other's journeys" (p. 19). Miller's guidance resonates with how I approached my students in my classroom as well as in my data, and beyond. Indeed, such an approach is a way of being in the world that I strive to embrace and embody, with varying degrees of success.

The Book

I begin with chapters focused on student talk about sexual and gendered identities, respectively, topics expected to be foregrounded in an LGBTQ+-themed literature course. In the chapter focused on sexual identities, I examine how movement among one another and the communities students embody and embrace is influenced by their conceptualization of coming out, their interrogation of labeling, and their experiences with and understandings of internalized homophobia. Moreover, I show how both movement and firm stances can be ethical or not. In the chapter focused on gendered identities, I delve into how students moved around and in trans and gender-fluid communities by interrogating the notion of normal as they read and discussed literature and lives in the classroom and in the school. I also look at cisgender young men and their experiences of gender, as represented by talk in classroom encounters. In doing so, I show how movement toward can be ethical, while stances away from an other can be unethical.

I then turn to student talk about race and religion, topics that bumped up against and overlapped with each other as well as with other identities in significant ways throughout the classes, as they were, in Winnubst's words, mutually constitutive. In the chapter on race, I concentrate on how white people pushed people of color away and how Black people pulled themselves toward the embrace of Black communities. I attend to differences, tensions, and power dynamics within racialized communities, including those we read and discussed as well as those we lived. As a result, this chapter shows students struggling with racist and antiracist ideas as they moved among one another. It complicates both the notion of movement and of what counts as ethical. I then look at movement in relation to religion. Christianity was discussed the most, with Catholicism in particular being foregrounded at times. Islam, too, was discussed, but in much less detail. Students talked about their experiences moving farther away from religious people when they embodied homophobic and trans-phobic values and closer to religious people when they embodied loving and accepting values. This chapter looks at students moving between what Ahmed calls homes and their experience of the loss when they have to choose and the gain when they do not.

I then move to the chapter focused on the ways students moved closer to and farther from their families, particularly their parents, as we wrote about and discussed families in the literature we read together and in the stories of our lives that we shared with one another. In this chapter, I explore how students critique, try to understand, and even come to appreciate families, particularly parents. In critiquing, they moved farther away, and in understanding and appreciating, they moved closer to their families and parents at various moments in time. This chapter shows how movement in opposition can be ethical. In the sixth and last data-driven chapter, I consider how giving, as distinct from forgiving, moved people closer to one another, which allowed for and even invited more "ethical encounters" (Ahmed, 2000) in the LGBTQ+-themed classroom. The book concludes by revisiting the driving questions as well as the scholarship, both empirical and theoretical, to which it strives to contribute. Ultimately, this book asserts the importance of moving and giving in making class-room encounters—really, all encounters—ethical ones. Finally, there is an appendix that delineates the methods of data collection and analysis for this study.

Chapter 1

Moving with Respect to
Sexual Diversity in Classroom Encounters

Students moved away from and toward sexual diversity as they read, wrote, and discussed LGBTQ+-themed texts in our shared literature classes. They were fairly comfortable navigating this terrain. They had elected to take a course on LGBTQ+-themed literature. They had elected to attend a charter school that actively and successfully recruited queer kids, including at events like the local Pride parade. But they were also of a generation whose set of experiences prepared them for such navigation. Their hometown had a Pride parade every year of their lives and many years prior. The "Don't Ask, Don't Tell" policy was instituted before they were born. Their state's Defense of Marriage Act passed in their lifetime, but they would not have been old enough to remember it. They could have recalled, though, the surge of queer youth suicides across the nation around 2010 and the contested response of the It Gets Better Project. And they knew that their state upheld the ban on same-sex marriage in 2014 and that this was struck down by the Supreme Court decision in the case of *Obergefell v. Hodges* in June of 2015, between the first and second semesters of the class. That they were capable of navigating movement among sexual identities, then, is perhaps not surprising.

As I talk about this movement, I draw on a distinction made by Lovaas, Elia, and Yep (2006) between LGBT studies and queer studies. They argue that LGBT scholars tend to characterize sexuality and gender as stable whereas queer theorists aim to "continuously destabilize and deconstruct the notion of fixed sexual and gender identities" (Lovaas et al., 2006, p. 6). Being queer, then, allows for more movement than being

LGBT. One might move from LGBT to queer, or vice versa, but within an LGBT way of being there is little to no movement, and within a queer way of being there is an infinite possibility of movement.

While the focus of this chapter is sexual identities, it is not sex, per se. I use the word *sex*, instead, to reference a characteristic of females, people who are intersex, and males. I do not use it to reference people's gender, like being a woman, a man, transgender, cisgender, gender-fluid, gender nonconforming, genderqueer, and such. I try very hard, in this chapter and in the book more broadly, not to use the word *sex* when I mean *gender* and vice versa. I talk more about this in the next chapter, but I mention it here, in this chapter on sexual identities, so you will understand why I use scare quotes when I use *"same"* before *sex* or *gender* to describe desire, as in *"same"-sex desire* or *"same"-gender desire*. I do this because when sex and gender are understood as on continua rather than as dichotomies, when they are understood as multiple and variable, or at least having that potential, as I understand them, then the chances of any one person experiencing and embodying these characteristics in exactly the same way at any given moment in time as someone else are quite slim. The idea of any two people sharing the same gender, then, is all but a fiction. The scare quotes are pointing to that fiction. So, this is how I use these words, knowing that other people use them differently. I am not trying to instigate a debate or meander down a rabbit hole. I am just trying to tell you what you need to know to understand what I am saying in this chapter. That said, I always strive to honor the language used by the students and the literature I reference above my own preferences. Using these parameters, I explore how the students with whom I shared LGBTQ+-themed literature courses moved both farther away from and closer to sexual diversity as they conceptualized coming out, as they considered and complicated the value of sexual identity labels, and as they grappled with the notion of internalized homophobia.

Conceptualizing Coming Out

In the spring of 2015, the class had just finished reading *Aristotle and Dante Discover the Secrets of the Universe*, and we were reflecting on the book. I had been reading, independently, an early draft of Darla Linville and David Lee Carlson's (2016) *Beyond Borders*. Thein and Kedley's (2016) chapter, "Out of the Closet and All Grown Up: Problematizing Normative

Narratives of Coming-Out and Coming-of-Age in Young Adult Literature," related to our reading of Ari and Dante, so I told the class about the chapter and said,

> [Thein and Kedley] posed these questions that I thought you might be interested in. So, they are kind of wondering about how a coming-out story—so if we understand that this is either Ari or Dante's coming-out story—is tied to the notion of growing up. The questions they ask, I will read them all, and then we can talk about them. How do coming-out stories reinscribe ideas of permanent sexuality that one must discover and accept? How do the narratives link growing up and coming out of the closet? In Ari and Dante, must Ari's love for Dante, or his desire in general, characterize Ari's sexuality as gay? Has Ari accepted his sexuality, or has he accepted his love for Dante, and what is the difference? Any thoughts on any of that?

This prompted a series of intertwined discussions with the students defining coming out, examining coming out in relation to *Aristotle and Dante*, and reflecting on their own experiences.

As they struggled to answer Thein and Kedley's questions, students worked to define what coming out was. One student offered a quick answer: "This is how I came out." Another pondered it, and a third, Corey, offered an example: *Blue Is the Warmest Color*. Although we had not read this book or watched this movie together, several people in the class had, and, together, they considered whether it was a coming-out story. One student, Parker, firmly asserted that it was not; Corey just as firmly repeated his assertion that it was. Parker asked Corey to explain, and Corey said, "Because it is about, I mean, it is a movie about a young woman discovering that she has—I do not want to say she is different, but she is discovering she is a lesbian, discovering that," and Sherry supported his claim, saying, "Because it starts out with her like with a boy, so." Here Corey and Sherry suggest that if a character is emotionally or sexually attracted to a person of the "opposite" gender, and then ultimately, in the story, the person is attracted to someone of the "same" gender, then this story is a coming-out story. Then Parker said, "But you keep using this word 'discovering,' and that word does not correlate with coming out. . . . I think coming out is an action rather than something internal. I think that you accept your queerness . . . and then coming out is telling other people around you in order for them to know who you are and feel comfortable with you. It is like when you sit people down and you are like, 'I am gay.' That is coming out." Thus, Corey and Parker discussed whether coming out described the process one goes through to discover one's sexuality or the process one goes through to tell others about their discovery.

Certainly, the two students brought very different life experiences to the conversation. Corey consistently identified as a white, cisgender young man, although he eventually told me, in our closing interview, that he had become bicurious. In contrast, Parker consistently identified as queer, at least in terms of sexuality, and more inconsistently and perhaps surreptitiously in terms of gender. In other words, at this moment in time, I cannot know whether Corey had come out to himself, but he had not come out to anyone else, whereas as Parker had quite broadly, including to family, friends, teachers, and staff, but also publicly, as Parker had written an article for a local queer magazine. Both ways of conceptualizing "coming out" were taken up in the proceeding discussion, and Jamie seemed to bring the two together when she said the following:

JAMIE: It is about the first crush that you realize is a crush.

DR. BLACKBURN: So, the first crush that you understand.

JAMIE: Where you can like, [say,] "I have a crush on this person."

The students did not land on a singular definition of coming out; rather, they grappled with the perhaps impossibility of doing so through examples in the literature we read and discussed and in their lives, about which they wrote and shared with the class.

There were, however, examples of coming-out stories all around us. Many of us had shared our own. Consider this one that Sherry had shared weeks prior. We were reading the first and second sections of *Aristotle and Dante*, and I had posed the following journal prompt: "Write about an experience that really challenged you or something with which you deeply struggled." Sherry offered to read her writing aloud to the class:

SHERRY: Okay, I grew up in a very, very Christian home, going to church since I was baby, and every summer since going to a [week-long camp] called [Local] Youth Camp. Around the time when I would go to camp was when I started discovering that I was gay. So when I went there, I would cry and pray and ask not to be this way. They taught that sin was horribly wrong and being gay was a huge sin. I could not help but feel horrible. Once there was another lesbian at the camp, and I got a crush on her, and she got a crush on me. We would pass letters back and forth, and I asked her how she was able to be gay and still feel comfortable, how she could come back to church camp and not be shut down. She told me it took her awhile, but she finally got there. I remember telling her that I could not be gay because God did not want that and I had to be straight for Him. This was right before I made out with her in the bathroom.

[*high five from Cobalt*]

[*laughter*]

DR. B: Very nice.

Sherry thus shared a version of a coming-out story, and it was a difficult one, full of shame. However, it was also one that was affirming in the moment, in that the girl whom she liked liked her back and demonstrated that affection. Further, it was affirming in the telling, in which a cisgender young man in the class high-fived her for having made out with the girl she liked and I responded to her story with "Very nice." In the moment of this coming out, Sherry seemed to have pushed away from gay ways of being, in keeping with her religion, and toward them, in acting on her desires. She seemed to have moved back and forth. By the time of this telling, though, she seemed solidly committed to being gay.

In talking about Ari and Dante, there was no question about whether Dante is gay. He comes out during the novel, so the questions became about Ari.

KIMBERLY: I guess the whole notion of, like, Ari accepting his sexuality versus accepting that he is in love with Dante—I think he is in love with Dante. I think he is not worried about his sexuality as much in this particular case because it is just like, it is Dante; of course he is in love with him. It does not matter that he is a boy. I mean, it does kind of a little bit, but, overall, it is just Dante. It is not necessarily, "I like boys" [but] "I like Dante."

DR. B.: Right, right, and the end kind of supports that, I think. Like, why would you ever be ashamed to love Dante?

PARKER: Right, it does not say, "Why would you ever be ashamed to be gay?"

DR. B.: Right, or to love boys. That is a good point. What about tying the growing up thing to the coming out thing? Or do you buy that Ari has come out? Brenda says no. Jamie is like, 'I am not sure.'

JAMIE: I am not even sure if Ari really has, like, a coming out. He is just kind of like—I feel like he does not need to, like, make the statement of "Oh, I am gay." It is just kind of like, "I love this guy." He has to be told that he loves him because he does not realize it for himself. I do not necessarily think that it is, like, a story of him coming out. It is him coming into himself.

DR. B.: So, like, the growing-up narrative trumps the coming-out narrative, if there is one?

JAMIE: Yes.

DR. B.: That one is the more prominent narrative, is the growing up.

JAMIE: Yes. Because it is not about him realizing he is gay. It is him growing up. It is him living his life.

Later in the same conversation, one student says, "I think [Ari] is Dante-sexual." As students talk together to figure out whether the novel is a coming-out story, they grapple with what coming out means and whether the main character does come out, and even whether he can come out if he is not gay but is instead "Dante-sexual." In doing so, they were working to understand the characters better, but they were working to understand themselves and one another better, too. They do not even accept the parameters of the questions. They work really hard to understand by pushing the boundaries out, by moving.

Throughout the conversation, students in the first class considered Ari's experience of (not) coming out in relation to their own experiences. Some students used their own stories to understand Ari's. Kimberly explained that she was like Ari in terms of not thinking she was gay until she had a crush on a girl. She said, "Well, I feel like that is kind of like what happened to me because I was like ten and I was like, maybe I am gay. I was like, no. I am not gay because that is just not me. I know other people are gay. That is cool. Then, like, I grew up a little more, and then I got a crush on a girl. I was like, 'Oh, okay.' So it is not necessarily that he is like, 'No, no, I am not gay.'" Kimberly drew on her experience to explain Ari as not homophobic or struggling with internalized homophobia but just not having experienced or noticed attractions to people of the "same" gender before Dante. Darby used her experience to wonder whether Ari ever identifies as gay. She said, "I think that Ari might not necessarily be, like, gay. It might be a Dante thing, because the first time that I ever, like, thought that I liked a girl, it was not like [an] 'oh my god, I am a lesbian' thing. It was a 'hey, this girl is really cute' thing. Maybe he is, but also we do not really know because the only guy that he has ever been like 'hm, I could kiss you probably' was Dante." Darby knew from her experience that being attracted to and sharing a relationship with one person of the "same" gender did not necessarily mean that someone was or was not gay. She applied that knowledge about herself to her understanding of Ari.

Other students used Ari's story to help understand their own. For example, Rhys, in talking about their own coming out, said, "I was so confused. . . . [I was] more in the stage of Ari . . . he is apparently a late bloomer because I was like in seventh grade, and I am a late bloomer. I liked this girl, but I did not really think about it. I look back, and I am like, 'Oh, great, I liked her.'" Rhys identified with Ari in terms of being older when they identified their attraction to someone of the "same" gender. In this way, coming to know Ari's story helped Rhys better understand their own.

Students also built on one another's stories to reflect on and develop their own. For example, after listening to Sherry, Kimberly said, "I was going to say something about what [Sherry] said about you do not realize that, like, your sexuality until you actually have a crush on someone, or something. I think that is, like, so true, because it is not really relevant in your life until you are actually interested in somebody. Then it becomes relevant. Like, 'Oh, these are the people I am interested in.'" In this way, Kimberly affirmed Sherry's description of her experience of "same"-gender desire and confirmed her memory of a similar experience.

Determining whether Ari is gay was no more the point than determining whether Kimberly, Darby, and Rhys were. It was irrelevant. What was relevant is how they used their life experiences to understand the characters and the novel better, used the characters in the novel to understand their lives better, and used one another's accounts to understand themselves and one another better.

Consider, then, the adaptation of Lovaas, Elia, and Yep's (2006) notion of LGBT studies and queer studies. Sherry stood solidly among LGBT people, particularly gay people, and Parker stood firmly in between there and queer people, considering both but not moving toward either. I understood them as standing apart from each other, but not far apart. Since both of them, and all of us in this class, were raised in a heteronormative and heterosexist if not outright homophobic society, as people who experienced "same"-sex desire, they likely had pasts that included unethical encounters in which their desires were negated if not threatened. They also likely had pasts that included the labor of having to get to where they were, where they could claim their desires and identities. So perhaps it is understandable that they were standing firm, determined not to be pushed from where they had worked so hard to get.

Kimberly, Rhys, and Darby had been raised in the same society but had experienced it differently, and, as a result, they moved. They pushed away from straight ways of being in the world, where they had been, and pulled themselves toward LGBT and/or queer ones. (If they were headed more toward one or the other—that is, LGBT or queer—it was not evident in this encounter.) In moving, they offered movement as an option for others in the class, including Sherry and Parker. They opened up potential future encounters for themselves and others through moving.

Valuing Labels

In talking about coming out, there were different estimations of the value of labels. Some students asserted that sexual identity labels were important to them. Simon, a white, trans young man, explained to the class that "there was always a misconception of, because I am trans, I am always, like, into girls and stuff, and that is annoying." He also said, "Now I identify, like, as a gay male." When I asked him why it mattered to him to claim a stable identity, at first he said, "I do not know. I do not know." Then, Rhys described their brother, who was trans and "identifie[d] as a gay guy." According to Rhys, "It just makes him really happy to, like, scream [his sexual identity] out in the living room that he is, like, doing something, 'I am gay.' It makes him so happy." So, Rhys did not say why claiming a stable sexual identity as a white trans man was important to Simon, but they told a story that let Simon know he was not alone. Then Parker said,

> Identifying has always been something that I have really strug-gled with, because I do not really see the point of it, but then again I do because if you are talking to someone and you tell them your identity, then there is no, like, blurred lines. They understand your intentions. They understand how far that they can go. That is where the friendship or relationship ends. It does not get complicated in that way, which is nice, because then you do not have be like, "Sorry, I don't like you." You have a reason to not like them. It is because you are not attracted [to] them in that sense.

Parker thus gave a reason why it might be important for "you," and by implication Simon, to claim a stable sexual identity. Rhys and Parker each offered a version of an answer to my question to Simon. It was only then that Simon answered for himself. He explained that while "saying one thing shouldn't be, like, just destiny," when he did not claim a stable sexual identity, he would "get hate from a lot of people."

Simon, as well as Rhys's brother, had to move to get from who he was assigned to be, who he was thought to be, to who he was. It is unclear whether the hate was in the previous metaphorical location or in the movement from it, but it seemed clear that the current location represented by a stable and alternative gender and sexual identity was a respite from that hate and that therefore he was reluctant to move from the current location, so he stood still by claiming particular gender and sexual identities.

Some students in the fall 2016 class also talked about the value of claim-ing particular sexual identities as they finished reading and discussing *Aristotle and Dante Discover the Secrets of the Universe*. The conversation was provoked when I asked, "Do you think that Ari is gay or just in love with Dante?" Students immediately said it did not matter, but then started labeling him. Vic said that while it didn't matter, she did not think he was gay because he is never shown "looking at some other dude." Mac pointed out that Ari expressed desire for two people, Dante and Alaina, a boy and a girl. So, I asked whether Ari was bi. Mac reiterated their belief that it does not matter. Since Ann initially asked whether Ari's sexual identity matters, I invited her to say more. She said, again, that it did not matter, but then said, "I actually think a really strong case could be made for Ari being asexual and demiromantic." I asked her to say more about that, and she said, "I actually marked on page 298 . . . 'Maybe kissing was part of the human condition. Maybe I wasn't human. Maybe I wasn't part of the natural order of things.' . . . That's so familiar to me, when it comes to struggling with coming to terms with my asexuality. And I think a lot of the ways he feels about his body and about his existence in space are something that I really identify with as someone who's asexual." In this way, students talked about how labeling Ari did not matter, but they went ahead and labeled him anyway; at least, Ann did. And not only did she label him, she labeled him with specificity far beyond that which is named in the book. Further, she labeled herself in relation to him.

This was not the first time that Ann self-identified as asexual. Nor was it the first time she relied on something we were reading in class to do so. Early in the semester, during our History and Poetry unit, we shared this interaction:

> ANN: I had no idea any of these poets experienced same-sex attraction at all. And I love these poets. I'm not a huge fan of Whitman, but I love Dickinson and I love Hughes. I've always identified with Emily Dickinson; I also want to "shut myself away in a house and write until I die." . . . That, that sounds very attractive. None of you people, no world to deal with, just being in the house, writing.

> DR. B.: Yeah, yeah. An introvert speaks.

> ANN: And I've been struggling a lot with my sexuality and my romantic orientation in the past few years, and it just blows my mind that nobody bothered to mention this in passing to me.

Although she did not specifically self-identify here, she stated that she had been "struggling a lot with [her] sexuality and [her] romantic orientation" and aligned herself with poets who had "experienced same-sex attraction," particularly Emily Dickenson, with whom she had "always identified." But just over a week later, we watched the film *Stonewall Uprising*, which is a documentary about the 1969 Stonewall riots. In response, Ann conveyed her terror at people who had experienced "same"-sex desire being treated with electroshock therapy, as if having a mental illness that required curing. In doing so, she implicitly self-identified as gay or asexual:

ANN: One of the things that terrifies me, because I can't tell you how many times my mom has said, "Hey, you should tell"—doctors, my, my therapist, or my psychiatrist, whichever mind doctor I'm meeting with that week—"you should tell doctor so-and-so that you're asexual or that you think you're gay or uncertain." It's like, "No I shouldn't."

DR. B.: Because you're afraid of what—

ANN: —they'll say.

DR. B.: Yeah, yeah. No, that's really terrifying.

ANN: Especially with asexuality, because there's a number of people who believe that that's a mental illness.

Here, Ann's focus was on her reaction to the film, and then she connected that to her own life experience. Then, not even two weeks later, when students were expected to share a project at the conclusion of the unit, Ann shared a sonnet she wrote:

> My lips are shaped for sin and meant for two
> At least that's what they tell me every day
> My mouth would shatter if I smiled, it's true
> But I am just a statue, a display
> A holy whore who watches from above

My teeth are carved on an eternal frown
I say there's nothing wrong with how I love
My heart and skin are not a battleground
I do not need your names, I have my own
I'm full of stories, I am full of song
I do not need your labels, or your robes
My porcelain is marble now—I'm strong
I know the things they say are never true
My lips are shaped for sin and meant for two

I understood the poem as about Ann's asexuality, but she did not plainly state that, and it was not taken up in that way by anyone in the class. But the next day, she talked about identifying with Ari in a conversation we were sharing about sexual identities and labels. In doing so, she explicitly self-identified as asexual. She said, "I identify as asexual right now. . . . [And] I started identifying as homoromantic." She then talked about the work labels did for her, much like Simon did, although the kind of work they did was quite different. Ann said, "I think, to me personally, I'm on the autistic spectrum. I'm really—I know 'high-functioning' isn't generally an accepted term, but I feel like it applies to me, so I use it when I'm referring to me. I'm really, really high-functioning, but I use labels as a coping mechanism, and so not having a label for some part of myself makes me feel like I'm missing something." In other words, Ann relied on labels to understand herself better.

Carter also described a similar need to claim a stable sexual identity. She said, "For the longest, I was like, 'Oh yeah, I'm bisexual,' but then, like, as time went on and, like, I, like, started learning more about the LGBT community and, like, learning all these different things, I was like, 'Woah, yeah, bisexual's, like, a thing, and, like, it identifies with me more than being straight, but . . . it doesn't get all the way there of, like, to who I am. Whereas, like, pansexual does, and being pan is, like, what I am, and it resonates with me." Carter claimed a label to represent her sexual identity because, like Ann, she thought it facilitated understanding, but, unlike Ann, she thought this was needed for others rather than herself. She said,

I think people just—we need—people are like, "Oh yeah, don't label," like, "we don't need labels" or "there's no reason for them," or "don't label people" or whatever, but then, in all technicality, like, we—we as a society need labels. Like, um, just to like, in general, be able to, like, function. Because, like, it makes life a lot easier to have something to call yourself or call something that you can't, like, fully explain, but, like, there's already an explanation there, and you can just use the word for it. Just simply, like, having like a title or a name for something just makes it a lot easier. So, like, I think that labels are, like, a necessity for us to have, just, like, as a coping mechanism for other people, so, like, other people, when they say, "Oh, I don't understand what you are," you can just easily say, "I'm this. This is the label that I identify with." Or, like, "resonate with" or whatever. And it just makes it a lot simple—like, just a lot simpler, for people to understand and stuff like that.

Simon, Ann, and Carter all found value in claiming labels to name their sexual identities to protect them from hate, to make themselves feel more whole, and to communicate more clearly with others. In this way, Simon's, Ann's, and Carter's moves to stability were similar.

But in other ways their moves were quite different. It could be argued that Simon moved toward a heteronormative way of being in the world, perhaps enjoying what Serano (2016b) calls "conditional cis privilege," or "passing privilege," in some contexts, whereas Ann and Carter moved within nonheteronormative ways of being in the world, from asexual to homoromantic, in Ann's case, and from bisexual to pansexual, in Carter's case. In doing so, it might be argued that they moved from one stable identity to another, thus only fleetingly experiencing queerness in between the stability of two LGBT ways of being, which is ironic, since none of their identities are represented in the LGBT acronym. By maintaining an openness to future fluidity, however, Ann and Carter were not fully outside of queer ways of being, which means they were still open to movement.

Complicating Labels

Ann's and Carter's openness to movement was evident. Even in the naming and claiming of sexual identity labels, Carter understood the importance of not being confined to one particular label. She said, "You cannot, like, you may not a hundred percent, like, confine yourself in that label or whatever, but, like, I don't know, like I'm pansexual, but I still have, like, my preference is more toward women than it is men, but yet I have a boyfriend. That doesn't make me straight and it doesn't make me a lesbian; that's like hopping over the line or whatever. But like, it just doesn't—it doesn't like—confine me either." Similarly, Ann left space for being able to change labels if she so desired. She said,

> Yeah, there's a chance that someday I'm going to meet someone and I'm going to want to have sex with them. I don't think so, but it's a possibility. You always have possibilities. And that doesn't—that wouldn't negate my sexuality now. That wouldn't retroactively make me a liar. . . . I started identifying as homoromantic because even though, like, I like guys and I find some guys attractive, I don't actually want to be in a relationship with a guy. But if I meet a guy I want to be in a relationship with, that doesn't make me less gay now. And it's a really important distinction that there's a difference between—it's okay to try on labels, and it doesn't make them wrong or inaccurate or lies or deluding yourself if that label changes.

In other words, claiming sexual identities at one moment in time did not mean, necessarily, that they would not change those identities either in the present, as with Carter, or in the future, as with Ann. That is, they did not understand being LGBT and being queer as mutually exclusive.

As mentioned above, Parker was conflicted about claiming sexual identity labels. They wondered whether young people should even bother coming out since they are likely to have so many different feelings and experiences across the years. They said,

> I think that [to claim sexual identity labels] is necessary in some ways, but in some ways, especially when you are still growing and still learning things about yourself, it is bad for you to limit yourself to those identities. Like, you should allow yourself for some swim room instead of, like, "I like girls, so I am gay." Then you stick yourself in this one box. If some really cool guy comes along or some trans guy or something, then you are like, "Oh my god, I am not allowed to like you, but I do." Then it is like coming out again. That was already difficult the first time. So why not wait until you figure yourself out in whole.

Darby immediately spoke up. She said, "I actually can speak to that because when I first, like, came out to my mom, it was like, 'I like girls. Okay, I must be gay.' Then, like, after that, I got kind of a crush on a boy, and I was like, well, I cannot just say, 'Hey Mom, I like a boy,' because she is going to feel like 'oh, you are lying.'" Here, Parker assumed that sexual identities fluctuate over time but would likely settle eventually. Their question was about why people claim identities during the fluctuation since reclaiming new and even former identities is difficult. Darby confirmed Parker's claim about this difficulty with an account of her own. Both expected to embody various sexual identities but also expected this variability to create difficulties for them, and Parker, at least, expected that their identities would stabilize over time. It is worth noting, however, that when Parker read a draft of this book, they commented specifically on this part, saying, "When I said 'I don't think young people should identify because they will feel stuck in it,' [these were] totally my dad's words. Thank goodness for independence ;-)," suggesting their evolving perspective on the issue and an opening up of a future that was different than what seemed possible when they were in high school.

Some students talked about how they wished such potential changes would be more easily accepted. Sarah, for example, offered this metaphor:

> This whole identity thing kind of reminds of a conversation I had yesterday with a four-year-old. [*laughter*] She is like, "Guess what I want to be when I grow up?" I am like, "I do not know, an astronaut." She was like, "No, a doctor, but then maybe I will be a chef. No, I want to be a chef, but I want to make, like, pastries but would never make it with nuts." She was going through all these jobs. That kind of reminded me about, like, identity. People expect you to be, like, young and have everything figured out, like know yourself perfectly. I just do not know. It is ridiculous.

Here Sarah suggested that to expect a single, stable sexual identity from an adolescent is "ridiculous." This resonated with Kimberly:

> KIMBERLY: That is, like, the perfect metaphor for identity. When we are little, we are like, "I want to be an astronaut." Then you are like, "I want to be a fashion designer." Then you are like, "I want to work in a bar like my mom." Then you are like, "No, I do not want to do that" when you look back on it.

DR. B.: What if you gave yourself that same freedom in terms of your sexual identity?

KIMBERLY: Exactly. 'Cause when you're like three and you are like, "I am going to be an astronaut," everyone is like, "Okay, you are going to be an astronaut," even though people are like, "No, you are not really going to be an astronaut."

Kimberly, among others, wanted the flexibility that young children have when imagining future careers for themselves. She valued the support they are offered, although the last phrase suggests that she valued that support even if it were not genuine, even if it were patronizing. The suggestion is, though, a preference for a queer community.

I never asked students to identify themselves in terms of sexuality in class. I listened closely to what they said, took notes, and then asked questions in interviews. In the first semester, though, when we read "Am I Blue?," a short story by Bruce Coville (1994), the question was posed. Sort of. The story is about a young man who is struggling to decipher his sexual identity and, in the process, gains a fairy godfather who gives him a kind of vision in which he sees anyone who has experienced any "same"-sex desire as slightly blue and anyone who experiences only "same"-sex desire as completely blue, and every hue in between. After we finished reading the story, Sherry said, "We should go around and tell everyone what shade of blue we'd be." Then, she started, "Okay. I guess I would be a dark sky blue. There we go." Then we went around the room, saying our shades and asking one another for more details:

PARKER: Before it storms? Like darkest blue you can get without being black? Right?

SHERRY: No . . .

DR. B.: I'm picturing Colorado skies?

SHERRY: Yeah. Like right before the sun goes down; like that kind of blue . . .

RHYS: I also have a picture of the sky turning, like, purple in my phone, which is in my—

DR. B.: Is that what color you are?

RHYS: No.

MOLLIE: Purple?

KIMBERLY: Purple.

DR. B.: Yeah? Tell me more.

KIMBERLY: I was like—I couldn't think of the right blue but then I thought of a purple and I was like that looks better. . . .

PARKER: Periwinkle or dark purple?

KIMBERLY: Periwinkle. . . .

RHYS: Shimmering blue; like you see me and just shimmering down my body blue, and it's like really radiant bright blue and shimmering. It's just like shimmering down. . . .

JAMIE: The [indecipherable] blue?

DR. B.: Oh, the color of the [hall] pass!

KIMBERLY: Yes. That's what I was thinking of, but more purple. . . .

DARBY: I feel like I would be like a mix between both shades of blue that my hair was because sometimes I'm probably gay and sometimes I'm probably not.

KIMBERLY: That's why I picked purple.

DR. B.: Does the red have any indicator in it or it's just not blue?

KIMBERLY: Just not blue. . . . It's purple. . . .

DR. B.: I like the idea of playing with depth of light, so I'm thinking of that water bottle blue. See how it's both dark and light because it allows light through it, but it's a darker color, so it's not like a turquoise water bottle but it's—

PARKER: It's really beautiful.

DR. B.: You are such a smart-ass. [*laughter*]

In this conversation, Sherry, Kimberly, Jamie, Darby, Rhys, and I self-identify in terms of blue as a metaphor for sexual identities. The story invites readers not to limit themselves to blue or not blue, as in gay or straight, but instead offers a continuum of shades of blue. Students accepted that invitation and then extended it, moving beyond blue, as Kimberly did, and complicating blue with light, as Rhys did. Here, movement seems playful, experimental, almost without consequence. Students tried on a future without necessarily leaving a past behind. They moved together, in some ways but not all ways. Students moved themselves toward a queer way of being without necessarily leaving an LGBT one behind.

(Externalizing) Internalized Homophobia

But not all movement was so joyful. Students also explored the concept of internalized homophobia, which describes when gay or lesbian people learn that not being straight is a bad thing and apply this belief to themselves. People who have internalized homophobia have moved fervently away from LGBT and queer ways of being in the world and forced themselves toward straight ones. Students explored this concept in our discussions of literature we read, particularly *If You Could Be Mine* (Farizan, 2013), *Aristotle and Dante Discover the Secrets of the Universe* (Sáenz, 2012), and "Am I Blue?" (Coville, 1994).

If You Could Be Mine provided us an opportunity to explore the idea of internalized homophobia. The novel, which is set in contemporary Tehran, begins as a love story between Sahar and Nasrin. On this day, we had just read chapters seven through nine. In the seventh chapter, Sahar takes Nasrin to a café that caters to LGBTQ+ people, where her cousin Ali is a "special customer" (Farizan, 2013, p. 88). Nasrin does not seem to notice the other customers until Ali "motions to a neighboring table. Two older women sit with each other, and even though they are not touching, the love in their eyes for each other is evident" (Farizan, 2013, p. 94). When Nasrin "looks at the women" (Farizan, 2013, p. 94), she gasps, looks "mortified" (p. 95), and "starts hyperventilating" (p. 95). As Sahar tries to calm her, she says, " 'No one cares who we are in here' " (Farizan, 2013, p. 95). Nasrin gets angry and says, " 'What do you mean who we are?' " (Farizan, 2013, p. 95), as if she has not been engaged in a romantic and sexual relationship with Sahar for a long time. At this point in our read-aloud of the chapter, Katherine blurted out her thoughts:

> KATHERINE: Nasrin is being super homophobic. I feel like it's the internalized homophobia, too. I don't know; it just blows my mind. . . .

> DR. B.: I can't believe she got so, her reaction was so strong to the two elderly women.

> KATHERINE: I think it's because she knows, on the inside, that's her and Sahar, but she's not really—I don't know if she's ready to accept it. Like, I know she loves Sahar, I think she feels that way, but she's not ready to take that step and making it, I don't know, public, or just being, "Okay, I'm never going to be married to a man; it's just going to be Sahar and I, but we'll never have kids." You know? "We'll never be able to, like, inherit our family's money," you know, "we might have to be living in the streets."

Katherine recognized Nasrin's actions as homophobic immediately and quickly applied that recognition to internalized homophobia. Nasrin's panic at being surrounded by LGBTQ+ people and horror at seeing Sahar and herself in the elderly lesbian couple in the café reveal her internalized homophobia. Nasrin's internalized homophobia provokes her to push herself out of an LGBTQ+ way of being in the world, which is clear when Sahar suggests they are a part of the surrounding LGBTQ+ community and Nasrin vehemently rejects this suggestion and asserts that they are apart from that community, not a part of it.

The next person to speak was Carter, who recognized not only Nasrin's internalized homophobia but also Sahar's. There is evidence of this in the eighth chapter, where Sahar says, "I know how I feel when Nasrin walks in a room. I feel weak and strong. I feel proud and ashamed. I feel love for her and hate for myself. I want to be clean of my feelings for her because they are wrong. Everyone knows that" (Farizan, 2013, p. 105). Carter recognized Sahar's shame and self-hatred as internalized homophobia and named it as such. In this excerpt of the book, Sahar pushes herself away from at least a lesbian way of being by saying, "I want to be clean of my feelings for her because they are wrong," thus judging this way of being and wanting to rid herself of it.

Both Nasrin's and Sahar's movement away from LGBTQ+ ways of being are propelled by internalized homophobia. They have been raised to believe that loving someone of the "same" gender is wrong, and they feel great shame and self-hatred because of their love for each other. Devastatingly, and oxymoronically, they are both experiencing the same thing together in total isolation. They are moving, but in ways that damage them, at least at this point in the story.

Aristotle and Dante Discover the Secrets of the Universe also provided us with opportunities to explore internalized homophobia, particularly in a scene that students called "the bath scene," which is in the eighth chapter of the third section. In it, Ari is in two full leg casts, and, since the novel is set in the eighties, the casts are plaster. As a result, Ari cannot shower or take baths, and his parents give him sponge baths, but in this chapter Dante offers to give him a bath, and Ari reluctantly agrees. It is an intimate scene, one that brings Dante to tears, which infuriates Ari. Ari says, "I wanted to yell at him. . . . all I wanted to do was put my fist through his jaw" (Sáenz, 2012, p. 144). In the first semester, students were to read the scene for homework before this conversation, but then Parker raised the topic:

PARKER: Wait, can we talk about the bath scene?

DR. B.: Let's talk about the bath scene.

PARKER: What the hell?

DR. B.: Chapter 8. What was going on?

PARKER: "Can I bathe you today?" Let's read it. Chapter 8.

Dr. B.: All right, let's go, chapter 8, which is page 143. This is, he has come back from the hospital. He has got two casts from ankle to thigh. He is moody and angry. He is kind of hating everybody right now.

In both of the semesters that we read this book, students were taken aback by this scene. They wanted to think through it together and even read it together, as they did here. So, we read the scene aloud together. Then, I initiated the conversation:

Dr. B.: So, what is going on there?

Parker: Sexual tension.

Dr. B.: There is a sexual tension. How is Ari feeling about the sexual tension?

Parker: Pissed off.

Dr. B.: Right, right. Why do you think he is pissed off?

Parker: Because he says he wants to hit him.

Dr. B.: Well, no, that is why you know he is pissed off. Yeah, you know he is pissed off, absolutely. But where is the, like, can you figure out where the anger is coming from? Why does it piss him off?

Sherry: It is because he doesn't know what's going on inside his brain.

Parker: Oh my god.

Dr. B.: Right, he is confused by it.

Parker: Okay, so that, but he is also kind of realizing that maybe he does have feelings for Dante and he does not like that. I think maybe the reason he did not want to talk about the accident and seem like a hero [was] because he does not want anyone to think, "I did it because I love Dante."

Here, Parker and Sherry, both of whom identify themselves as queer, albeit differently, not only from each other but also at different times and places, scrutinized the scene and tried to understand Ari's anger. Both of them seem to interpret Ari as coming to recognize his desire for Dante, but it was Parker who plainly stated, "[Ari] does have feelings for Dante and he does not like that." In that, we see Parker's recognition of Ari's internalized homophobia. We also see, in the "bath scene," Ari violently pushing himself away from experiencing "same"-sex desire, specifically desire for Dante, even if only in his imagination.

This violent pushing away from what is understood as gayness is material in Bruce Coville's "Am I Blue?" Recall that this short story is about Vince questioning his sexual identity with the support of his fairy godfather. One of the people in Vince's life is Butch, who routinely beats up Vince because he perceives Vince as gay. Ultimately, we learn that Butch is gay. At this point in our reading of the story, Delilah said, "I had a feeling that was going to happen . . . The—his bully was also gay . . . because like, you know, like sometimes, like, when people make other people, like, down or whatnot, it's because the other person that they're bullying has something that they want or something that they are; they just don't know how to get their feelings out. So it makes them hurt other people." Here, Delilah suggested that Butch abuses Vince either because he desires him or because he sees his own "same"-gender desire in him. This was almost four weeks after we talked about internalized homophobia in *If You Could Be Mine*, so I reminded her, "Remember when talked about internalized homophobia? So we see that Butch has this internalized homophobia that he's taking out on Vince, right?" Thus, I underscored what they had learned about the concept of internalized homophobia.

When Sahar sees "same"-gender desire in herself, she is ashamed and hateful, but toward herself. When Nasrin, Ari, and Butch see this desire in themselves, they take it out on others. In other words, they externalize their internalized homophobia, although they do so differently. Nasrin does so verbally, Ari does so in his imagination, and Butch does so violently. All of them, to different degrees, though, push themselves away from lesbian or gay ways of being in the world and pull themselves toward straight ones, even homophobic ones, at least for these focal moments in time. Students reflected on their own experiences with such pushing and pulling in mind.

Mac told a story about their brother. Before he came out, according to Mac, "everyone would pick on him for being gay." Thus, he learned that being gay was something that prompted abuse. Then, after he came out, he started calling Mac a lesbian and a dyke, even though they did not identify as such at the time. According to Mac, "it always had, like, a negative connotation to it, so that made me like, 'Oh no, is this,' like, I never thought that being gay for anyone else but myself was bad. I felt like if I was gay, that would be bad. . . . Yeah, that's, um, that's why for awhile I was like, 'No, I'm straight.' . . . And that's why I was trying to prove him wrong by having a lot of boyfriends. . . . And I felt like I had internalized homophobia." In other words, Mac's brother internalized homophobia and then taught Mac to do the same by externalizing his homophobia onto Mac. In this way, both Mac and their brother pushed themselves away from gay and lesbian ways of being and pulled themselves toward straight and homophobic ones, at least for moments in time. When movement is provoked by hatred, whether the movement is away from that which is hated or toward that which is not, the movement is not ethical, and it has harmful consequences, whether for the person moving, for those around them, or both.

Isolation and Internalized Homophobia

In the next chapter, I discuss at some length a young man I call John and his deep investment in being not just a cisgender but also a masculine man. Of course, being a cisgender and masculine man does not mean being a straight man, but it was how I understood him. In fact, that's how he explicitly identified in our concluding interview. But in his journal, when he wrote about the turmoil of his life before coming to this school, his struggle getting into any high school, and then the orientation for this school, he went on to write, "That's when you spot him, He's tall, slim, with blonde/brown hair, blue eyes. You sit next to him, his eyes light up. . . . 2 months and we're inseparable." Then he described the two of them coming back from a game of "airsoft," stripping down to their boxers, and embracing each other: "You cling to him and [he] clings back, locked in a loving embrace." He prefaced the account by saying, "There is no shame between you two," and concluded it by saying, "But neither of you are ashamed." In other words, the account is framed in shame, but a rejection of shame. Then he offers a sort of epilogue for the story, beginning with "2 years later." The epilogue references the "one awkward time where you went camping and the showers were just one big line and you get it." Then, about a month later, when we were discussing the bath scene in *Aristotle and Dante Discover the Secrets of the Universe*, John said, "But I mean, I've taken a—I've taken a bath with one of my friends before. You know, we got back from four days out of airsoft and we were all dead tired. And I'm just, 'I'm going to get in the shower.' And I looked at the water heater, because it had a little meter on it that says how much is left, and I'm like, 'Oh crap.' And I'm like, 'Want to hop in the shower with me?'" This account could be understood to fill in some of the blanks of that early journal entry. The embrace happened after "airsoft" and the shower much later, in the journal entry, and there are other variations, but still the experience of intimacy with a friend who also identifies as a young man was consistent across both of John's stories. A significant difference between the two, though, is that the journal entry was, as far as I know, private, and the comment public. I did not understand this public telling to be a coming out for John, though. Instead, I heard him saying, "Dante can bathe Ari, and it doesn't mean either one of them is gay. I mean, I took a shower with a guy, and clearly I'm not gay." At this point in the book, readers do not know whether Ari is gay. I cannot know what John believed at this point. I know that John was very engaged in this book. He was reading ahead of the class and talking about literary devices used by the author, including foreshadowing. I also know that in the prewriting for his final essay in the class, he noted that "the LGBTQ+ part of [*Ari and Dante*] didn't get big until the last sections," that he preferred "where the narrators sexuality is shown early on," and stated, "I hate surprises." From this, I take it that John did not expect Ari to fall in love with Dante and felt a bit surprised by this turn of events at the end of the novel. This is quite different than how I understood that early journal entry, in which I did not understand him to come out, but I did understand him to be embracing intimacy between two men. Thus, in the private context, John stood near men who love men, but in the public one, in a classroom encounter, he stood farther away from such men. In neither context did I see him move from one position to another. Like with Simon earlier in this chapter, I understand John's standing still as about safety, wanting to be safe, but rather than having worked really hard through the hate to get to safe, as Simon had, I understand John as just not willing to take the risk at all.

Ethical Movement with Respect to Sexual Diversity in Classroom Encounters

Sometimes students moved with respect to sexual diversity in classroom encounters, and sometimes they did not. Students stood still among communities that they had worked hard to get to and were not eager to leave. Students moved deliberately and carefully, crafting lives for themselves. Students also moved playfully from one community to another, exploring possibilities for themselves in the present and future. I saw these stances and moves as empowering and ethical.

But not all stances and moves were. Students talked about characters who moved in ways that were provoked by and perpetuated hate, which led to a conversation about a family member doing something similar. So, it was not that the students moved with animosity, or unethically, at least not in the context of the class, but they recognized when others did. In the class, though, one student took a troubling stance. Rather than move toward men who love men, as he did in the privacy of his journal, he stood with heteronormativity, even in this LGBTQ+-themed class in this queer-friendly school, even with all of his white, cis, male privilege. A stance can be ethical when it is preceded by movement and when it holds the possibility of being followed by movement. A stance can be ethical when it remains agile. But a stance without movement before or after lacks the opportunity to encounter others. Such a stance is one of isolation, reification, ossification. It is not ethical. Movement is needed to encounter others; it is not *all* that is needed, but it is *always* needed. Sometimes those encounters are harmful, and sometimes they are empowering, even joyful. The difference is in whether they are agile, whether they are ethical.

Chapter 2

Moving with Respect to
Gender Diversity in Classroom Encounters

Although students were somewhat practiced at negotiating sexual identities, they were less practiced at negotiating gender expressions and identities. They were not alone. Whereas being lesbian and gay were removed from the American Psychiatric Association's *Diagnostic and Statistical Manual of Mental Disorders* in 1973, long before any of these students were born, *gender identity disorder* was changed to the less stigmatizing *gender dysphoria* in 2013, when these students were teenagers. By the time our classes were meeting, though, Laverne Cox was famous for her role in *Orange Is the New Black* (Kohan, 2013–19), and *Transparent* (Soloway, 2014–2019) was a television series. Moreover, Caitlyn Jenner publicly disclosed her identity as a trans woman toward the end of the first class. As such, conversations about the complicated nature of gendered identities were beginning, but they still had (and have) a long way to go. For that reason, it is worth taking a moment to discuss some of the terminology I use in this chapter and in the book more broadly.[1]

Gender identity is "how an individual feels about themselves, intuits, and then writes themselves into the world"; gender expression is the "physical manifestation of one's gender identity" (Miller, 2019, p. 86). They are interrelated but not synonymous. Miller (2019) conceptualizes gender identity as both "trans-sectional" and "trans-cultural." This means that gender is always among multiple forms of identity, all of which are "in

---

1. The following three paragraphs are a modified excerpt from an article published in *Pedagogy, Culture & Society* (Blackburn, 2021).

perpetual deconstruction and construction and are identified by . . . indeterminate integration and ever-shifting amalgamation of identities" (Miller, 2019, p. 74). Moreover, "when complex gender identities move across different physical, material, and symbolic borders, they activate and fortify (although temporally) new gender identity formations" (Miller, 2019, pp. 75–76). This conceptualization of gender aligns with my experience with students in the LGBTQ+-themed literature course. This means that when I represent them in terms of gender, it is a partial representation, always, but it is also a tentative one.

I use the word *trans* as an abbreviation of *transgender*, drawing on Airton and Meyer's (2018) definition, to describe "individuals who blur the lines of binary gender identity or gender expression" (p. 322). I interpret this definition to include individuals who are "gender transgressive," or, in Serano's (2016a) terms, "downright 'breaking' the laws of gender" (p. 267). In keeping with the National Center for Transgender Equality (2016), I use the word as a "broad term . . . to describe people whose gender identity is different than the gender they were thought to be when they were born." I use *cisgender* to describe people whose gender identities are the same as the gender they were thought to be when they were born. These definitions are not universal; indeed, no language is, and certainly not language as contested as "trans-related terminology" (Serano, 2016a).

In describing each student, I use terminology as specific as possible to honor their differences from one another (Green, 2016). Moreover, I use language they use. This is complicated in that I have spent a lot of time with them; they described themselves in different ways over the course of a semester (not to mention in the years we have been in touch since). Another complication is that sometimes the words they used did not align with how those words are typically used, whether colloquially or academically. Reasons for this might be simple, like the vocabulary may have been new to them, or complicated, like they may have been struggling with internalized hatred. I can find myself getting dizzy on what Serano (2016a) calls the "Activist Language Merry-Go-Round" (p. 247). But, as she points out, the merry-go-round doesn't stop because we find the right language; it stops when the associated stigmas stop. In an effort to be a part of the work of destigmatizing trans identities and expressions, I forge ahead, cautiously, carefully.

As students languaged gender, they moved around and in trans-ally, gender-fluid, and trans communities. They read, wrote about, and discussed fiction, such as *If You Could Be Mine* (Farizan, 2013) and *Brooklyn, Burn-*

ing (Brezenoff, 2011); nonfiction, such as *Beyond Magenta* (Kuklin, 2014) and *Some Assembly Required* (Andrews, 2014); and the lives of those on a school-wide panel to discuss issues pertinent to trans people. Whereas sometimes they stood back and deciphered characters and people, trying to figure out their gender or maybe even sex (e.g., male, female, intersex), other times, they pulled themselves in to connect and to be allies or members of various trans communities. I examine such movement in this chapter, but I also take a look at an example of apparent stagnation, when a student stood firm as an immutably masculine man.

Trans Allies

That said, the effort of cisgender students to move themselves toward trans-ally communities and thus near trans people was something I saw across classes and across texts. This was evident in the third-semester class as we read and discussed the fourth chapter of *If You Could Be Mine* (Farizan, 2013). (For more on teaching this book, read Blackburn & Deiri, 2018.) In the chapter, Sahar, the main character and narrator, attends her cousin Ali's party, escorted by Ali's friend Parveen. While Sahar has been in a romantic and sexual relationship with her best friend, Nasrin, for a long time, this is the first time she has been in a social gathering of LGBTQ+ people. There is drinking, drug use, and dancing; Sahar is completely out of her element. Parveen proves to be a good friend while they are at the party, then Ali informs Sahar that Parveen is trans, which challenges Sahar to recognize and interrogate some of her transphobic ideas. In the class, students shared journal entries responding to this prompt: "Identify any line in chapters 1–6 that stands out to you. Write the line. Explain why it stands out to you."

Delilah selected a line from the end of chapter 4 where Parveen put her number in Sahar's phone, and when she returns her phone, their hands touch lightly. According to Delilah, "there's tension between them." Kristy added that after Sahar found out that Parveen was trans, "Parveen put her arm, like, around Sahar's shoulder," Sahar "stiffened," and Parveen removed her arm. These lines, identified by Delilah and Kristy, reveal Sahar's transphobic behavior toward Parveen. I named what I heard Delilah and Kristy to be suggesting: "The key to what you just said is 'after she found out,' right? So that when Sahar understands Parveen as a girl, she likes her, right? Not flirting, but likes her. And then when she finds out that she's a trans girl, her transphobia kind of starts flaring up. So she winces from her, she doesn't, you know, so that we see some evidence of transphobia in Sahar." Sahar's transphobia, however, needs not be permanent, as Kristy suggested with the line she selected, where Sahar says, "I take the mobile back and thank him. *Her*. Thank *her*. Damn it" (Farizan, 2013, p. 51). Here Kristy recognized in Sahar a self-awareness akin to her own. Kristy explained, "I think that's really important because people, like, who are accept—are like trying to accept a person as transgender, if they misgender them, they get really upset about it, and they try to—they like correct themselves immediately after, and then they constantly are like saying their new gender in their head to, like, not have that happen again, whether they say it to that person or just in their thoughts or something." In this way, Kristy recognized both Sahar and herself as cisgender people who get upset when they misgender trans people they are trying to accept and work deliberately to prevent doing so again. I underscored this trait of Sahar, at least, when I affirmed Kristy, saying, "Right. So we know that she has transphobia, but she's working on it, right?" Not only is Sahar working on it, so too was Kristy. In this way, together, we recognized Kristy, the student, alongside Sahar, the character, as moving from past encounters in which she struggled or even failed as a trans ally and moving toward future encounters in which she would embody trans allyship, recognizing that such movement requires ongoing effort, not one good step and done. It requires moving, deliberate movement. Such movement, then, opens up possibilities of trans allyship.

Lisa and Kristy practiced identifying transphobic ideas and behaviors in reading this novel. Lisa, for example, noticed Ali behaving in transphobic ways. She said, "I picked the line where Ali was like, 'Don't be so square, Sahar. Parveen's a transsexual.' I'm like, 'Really?' This made me really upset because I didn't like that Ali was telling Sahar Parveen's business without her permission. I was like, 'That's not cool.' . . . Also, at the same time, I don't like how he makes it seem like it's so obvious." Lisa critiqued Ali for disclosing Parveen's trans history and for belittling Parveen by suggesting she is not convincingly feminine, implying a trans ally like herself would not do either of these things. Kristy emphasized Lisa's point, saying, "that's what [trans people] work hard for, is so that they feel comfortable in the gender they want to be; it's not for you to be like, 'Oh, it's obvious.'" Here, Lisa and Kristy were struggling and striving to be trans allies while being outside of trans communities. They were not perfect allies; for example, one could judge Kristy for talking about what gender trans people *want* to be as opposed to *are*, but no one did, and I would argue that there is no such thing as a perfect ally. Still, Lisa and Kristy moved toward being allies by critiquing the shortcomings of Ali as a trans ally, at least in some moments in time. Thus, they moved toward trans-ally communities by metaphorically pushing against a character in whom they identified transphobic ideas and behaviors. In doing so, they opened up a future of possible encounters in which they embody trans allyship.

Similarly, Desiree critiqued Sahar for her superficial understanding of trans people. A significant part of the plot of the novel is that Sahar wants to transition to living as a man, not because she is a man or even feels like a man—she is not; she does not—but because she wants to marry her lover, who, like Sahar, is a woman. In the setting of this novel—in Tehran, the capital of Iran, around 2010—being transgender is considered an illness that needs to be cured. As such, gender-affirmation surgeries and other medical interventions are legal. In contrast, being gay or lesbian is considered illegal and therefore needs to be punished. This is why Sahar seriously considers transitioning. That said, from the perspective of students in the class, who have grown up in the twenty-first century in the United States, where being gay or lesbian is legal, even where it is understood to be immoral, transitioning just to be with the person you love seems impulsive and reckless; moreover, it seems to trivialize the experiences of transgender people. Desiree made this point when she shared the line she selected, which was when Sahar says, "There is so little time before the wedding. I don't really have time to decide whether I am making the right decision" (Farizan, 2013, pp. 76–77). After reading this line aloud, Desiree quickly critiqued Sahar:

> She's making the wrong decision, because every day people struggle with, like, the fact that they want to be a different gender, and I feel like she's doing it for the wrong reasons. And that just sits very uncomfortable with me, and I don't like it. Because there are people that struggle with this decision every day; you're just doing it because you want to be with the other gender. . . . I don't feel like you should change your sex or your gender because you just want to be with this person.

Desiree described the difference between Sahar and trans people in terms of what Sahar "want[s]" versus how trans people "struggle." In this way, she passionately articulated a problem with this plot element in the novel.

Further, she, like Lisa and Kristy, pushed off of a character to move herself toward trans allies, opening up a future of possible trans allyship.

Another plot element of *If You Could Be Mine* that raised issues of cultural rather than individual transphobia was about the roles of women and men in contemporary Tehran. Khalil wondered aloud how Parveen got to Sahar's house to escort her to the party. He said, "I'm kind of confused, because I'm like, 'So why did she travel by herself?'" Desiree explained that her AP Government class had recently studied Iranian "customs and . . . values" and that they had learned that "one woman is not allowed to go anywhere by herself." Kristy suggested that perhaps Parveen is still understood as a man even though she is a woman:

> Ali said that everyone knows about Parveen. So maybe because [transitioning is] legal, he said that it's legal and the government actually helps pay for it, because they want to help "fix" them, and so he says, like, everyone knows. . . . So like—well, my thing is I think that it's because everyone—or they might still see Parveen as the male, so like—or even though they see her as a female, they know she used to be a male, so they think she has the capacity to take care of herself. I don't know. It still should be like even if she has that transition, she still should not be out by herself.

Here, students grappled with understanding a contemporary story set in a very different city and country than their own, one they had studied but not experienced. Simultaneously, they struggled with values that they had learned to be both sexist and transphobic to understand a plot element.[2] Thus, the students recognized they were quite far away from Parveen in some ways, including geographically and nationally, but they were simultaneously pulling themselves toward her in terms of gender, both as a woman and as a trans woman. Although no one in the conversation identified as a trans woman, they pulled themselves *near* trans women as they tried to understand their experiences better—that is, as they tried to earn their places in trans-ally communities. In doing so, they moved

---

2. It is possible that this particular plot point is simply an authorial oversight, which might be explained by the fact that Farizan grew up in the United States. Her parents were born and raised in Iran, but she was not; therefore, she might not have thought through this detail.

themselves farther away from past encounters when they perhaps enacted transphobia and closer to future encounters when they might be more likely to enact trans-positive behaviors.

Gender Fluidity

As described in the introduction, *Brooklyn, Burning* (Brezenoff, 2011) is a novel in which neither the main character, Kid, nor the love interest, Scout, is identifiable in terms of sex or gender. We read and discussed the book in the first-semester class, and Kid's and Scout's sex and gender were the topic of many of our discussions about the book, including a conversation shared with the author after finishing the book (for more on this, read Blackburn & Schey, 2018).

Many times in these discussions, students stood back and deciphered the characters, struggling to ascertain their sex and gender. For example, Parker wondered aloud, "I'm just curious if the fact that Kid is living on the streets, and there's, like, a stereotype of surviving on the street that comes with masculinity and strength—you know, I wonder if that part of Kid plays into Kid's gender." Parker suggested that Kid is a young man as evidenced by their living on the streets. I understood Parker as talking specifically about gender, as distinct from sex, which I underscored by saying, "Right. Like the performance of gender is, in part, a protection device." But then Parker either clarified that they were talking about sex rather than gender or used the words interchangeably, saying, "Like would it be more difficult for Kid to live away from home in this warehouse if Kid were a female? Because like then they're subject to different dangers, you know." Rhys clarified Parker's point, saying, "girls are normally more common to be, like, to, um, fear males." Here, students talked about Kid, trying to figure out their sex and gender by analyzing the way they behave in particular contexts, like the streets, and in response to other characters, particularly men. They drew conclusions, albeit not definitive ones, based on their interpretations.

Other times, students again just stood back and watched, but instead they let go of the need to figure out either the sex or gender of the characters. Consider, for example, this interaction:

COREY: [Their sex and gender has] just [been] open throughout the story. But I honestly don't—I mean, while I do think that,

I don't think the fact that it's not gendered changes anything about it, because we're all just people. I don't think gender really changes anything, is what I'm saying.

JAMIE: I think that's the point.

COREY: I think we're all just people.

JAMIE: I think that's the point. A lot of people get too hung up on gender, hence the reason that it is gender-neutral, because everyone—people are just people, and it makes it easier for people that are so hung up on that to just get into it. . . .

RHYS: So, that's how I'm going through it. I'm just like, whatever. I don't care; I don't even need that information.

Here, three students, one of whom identified as a cisgender man, another who identified as a cisgender woman, and a third who experimented some with gender, stated that gender does not matter because "we're all just people." You can hear an adapted-to-gender color-blind mentality echoing through these comments, which is what I think Parker was hearing when they said, "What if they're trans, though. . . . That's what [Simon] and I keep discussing." It's worth mentioning that Simon had already disclosed his trans identity to the class and Parker had, just that day, at the start of the class, said this:

PARKER: I have an announcement.

DR. BLACKBURN: What? You have an announcement?

PARKER: Yeah.

DR. B.: I want to hear it.

PARKER: Today is, like, I am going to gender therapy for the first time.

DR. B.: Hey, congratulations. Oh, that is great, yay. Where will you go?

PARKER: Somewhere in [local] hospital.

DR. B.: Excellent, excellent, and will it be after school or during school?

PARKER: Yeah, well, during school, but I get to leave early.

DR. B.: Oh, I hope it goes wonderfully. Let us know, if you are comfortable with that. Congratulations. That is big.

Thus, Parker communicated that they were actively pursuing questions around gender; further, they were publicly affirmed for doing so. So perhaps it was not surprising that Simon and Parker's classmates took up their question, saying, "Oooh," suggesting that was a new thought coming from arguably the only trans students in the class. This new thought marked a place of movement. One that surprised me because I always assumed Kid was trans. I figured the students shared my assumption, but their reaction to Parker's comment suggested otherwise.

Parker's suggestion opened up possibilities and thus challenged students to step into the story to get to know the characters, rather than to decipher them or just let them be. Rhys, for example, immediately after, considered these possibilities: "I think that Scout's more feminine, and then I think that Kid is more masculine. So we can kind of stick them on a gender spectrum. But they could very well be, like, Scout could be female-bodied or not, Scout—Scout can be like male-bodied and Kid could be female. It's just we don't know." Here, Rhys deliberately separated sex and gender and thus strove for a more complex understanding of Kid and Scout. Then Jamie suggested that Kid might be gender-fluid:

JAMIE: I think Kid might want to be gender-fluid. And like, go back and forth.

DR. B.: What makes you think that?

JAMIE: . . . I think they want to be fluid because they have feminine qualities and they have masculine qualities that they don't want really—I don't think they lean necessarily more toward one or the other fully?

DR. B.: That's supported by the dad's response, right? "You need to decide." Or "you need to make the choice" or something.

JAMIE: Yeah, yeah.

Following Rhys's lead, Jamie observed Kid's "qualities," rejected dichotomous notions of gender to describe them, and instead opted for "gender-fluid." Parker's comment seemed to invite that possibility. Such an effort relied less on stereotyping than the deciphering approach did and more on engagement than the we're-all-just-people approach did. Thus, spending time with, in this case, characters and getting to know them allowed for movement toward, a connection.

I saw this even more so in the second semester. We did not read the book as a class, but several students read it independently, and sometimes we talked about it before and after class. Mac acknowledged that it was "hard to decipher" the gender of Kid and Scout, but when I asked whether this bothered them, they said, "No, I'll figure it out. . . . I know that there's probably a reason for it that they intentionally did." Not only did it not seem to bother Mac, they seemed to really enjoy the book and all of its gender ambiguity. When I initially asked who was reading it, Mac was the first to respond:

DR. B.: Anybody reading *Brooklyn, Burning*? Just because I'm curious. How's it going?

MAC: It's going really good.

DR. B.: Is it, you like it?

MAC: I'm reading it and I'm just like—Bae. Kid is bae.

DR. B.: Aww.

MAC: So is Scout. And Felix. And Fish.

DR. B.: Yeah.

MAC: Everyone.

DR. B.: Oh good, oh good. Yeah, I think everyone has—you can see the good in a lot of people.

In addition to reading and enjoying it, they drew a bookmark of a significant character (see figure 1). Recall that Mac was engaging with this book entirely of their own choice and on their own time. And with the

Figure 1. Mac's illustration of Felix in Brezenoff's (2011) *Brooklyn, Burning*.

way they were imagining the characters, they were building community with them, as people who experience gender fluidly. That is to say, Mac, who identified as white, moved within gender-fluid communities as they embraced the characters in the novel. Rather than moving toward trans-ally communities, like some other students had, or even toward trans communities, Mac was unique in moving among others like themselves, even if those others were characters in a novel.

Interrogating Normal

It was in the first few weeks of the first semester's LGBTQ+-themed literature course when I noticed some students were using the word "normal" when what they meant was cisgender. I had failed to call them out on the spot, so when *normal* was used similarly in the book we were reading, Susan Kuklin's (2014) *Beyond Magenta: Transgender Teens Speak Out*, I raised the issue. The book is a collection of photo essays focused on six different teens. We were discussing Nat's story, entitled "Something Else." Nat uses they/them/their pronouns and describes themself as intersex. The first sentence of their story is, "How can I explain myself to some-one normal?" (Kuklin, 2014, p. 121). When we discussed the story as a class, I said, "I also noticed that [Nat's story] started off with them using the same thing we fell into last week of the *normal* versus *cisgender*, like, 'How can I explain myself to someone normal?'" The initial student response was one of pity; Kimberly said, "It is kind of sad like reading trans stories when they say things about, like, normal people because it implies that they feel like they are abnormal . . . I mean. It's like, 'Aw, it's okay.'" Here, Kimberly moved herself near and perhaps a bit above Nat but not with Nat.

Then, though, there was an extended conversation about the word and concept of *normal*. Cobalt said, "There is no such thing as normal"; Kimberly suggested it was a "social construct." Cobalt and Jamie mentioned that it was used in "hurtful" and "derogatory" ways. Then several students considered normal as relative; Darby described it as having "mostly . . . to do with what environment you are in," and Parker extended this to time periods. Corey said Hunter S. Thompson predicted that weird would eventually become normal, quoting him as having said, "When the going gets weird, the weird turn pro." Sarah then brought the conversation back around to LGBTQ+ people. She said, "I think it is weird. There has been

LBGT people for since people began, like they always been there, but like now it is just starting to be considered, like, normal, but they have just always been there." Here, Sarah moves herself near LGBT people, and not above, as Kimberly did with trans people, just near. I explained that there has always been same-sex desire and diverse gender expressions but that the terms *lesbian, gay, bisexual,* and *transgender* are comparatively recent. Then I said, "It is interesting when the behaviors get named and how that defines normal and not normal. It draws a line between normal and not normal. I think *LGBT,* as you point out, kind of does that work. It can mark people." Here, I moved myself more closely with queer communities than LGBT ones by pointing to how in claiming and assigning sexual and gender identities people mark themselves and are marked by others in relation to normalcy.

Moving around and in Gender-Fluid Communities

Cameron is one of the six teens in Kuklin's *Beyond Magenta;* in some ways, their story is the most prominent. Cameron is featured on the cover of the book, wearing a pink button-down, jeans, a black bow tie, a rainbow belt, earrings, and a digital watch. Throughout their chapter, there are twelve full-page color images, which is much more than any other teen's section. Cameron appears in skirts in some of these photos, ties in others, jeans and T-shirts in others.

When we discussed Cameron's story in the second-semester class, students began with confusion. In the first thirty lines of a 150-word encounter, students used some derivation of the word *confuse* five times and *contradiction* three times. Carter said, "They seriously confuse me. Like, like because . . . not like serious contradictions, but like, some contradiction in what they say. It's kind of confusing." Katherine and Yanika reiterated Carter's sentiment. Together, they seemed to be trying to decipher who Cameron was. Mac, who identified as gender-fluid, said this:

> That's also something; it was like, he did—and it was like, "yeah I identify as a guy," but I don't think he ever—or they ever, you know, touched on the fact that they were gender-fluid. Like they briefly brought it up, like, "I mix, like, my outfits—I'm a little bit feminine, a little bit masculine," but they never really talked about coming out as, like, gender-fluid . . . I don't know,

I just—I wanted to hear about that, because they do prefer they/them/their, so I wanted to hear about how they, you know, they were already saying that they were questioning, you know, gender roles, but they never went into the specific of "oh, I'm gender-fluid." . . . I would have just liked to hear about that.

Mac's comment marks a sort of shift in the encounter, when students started trying to connect with rather than decipher Cameron and their experience.

For example, Carter connected to Cameron's account of coming to school and asking everyone to call them by their name and to use their pronouns. Cameron said people mostly adjusted, but "I had some issues with two teachers, that didn't make a whole lot of sense to me because they never knew me as a girl, so why would they call me *she*?" (Kuklin, 2014, p. 114). Carter related to this because she changed the name by which she was addressed when she came to the school. She said,

Since I've been here or whatever, most people, like, people who knew, uh, who have known me outside of me going here, like, they, uh, they call me by my actual first name or whatever, but then there's people here that I've met, like, just here or whatever, so they know me by [Carter] . . . but sometimes, like, people will call me, like, my first name. And it's like "what are you doing, . . . you don't know me outside of school," like, so for people who've known me before, I'm like cool with you calling me by my first name, but like, if you haven't, then we have a problem because you met me by this name, so why are you calling me something I did not tell you to call me?

Having made this connection, Carter no longer expressed her confusion or pointed to Cameron's contradictions. Mac built on Carter's story, saying,

It's like when people call me by my first name. It's like, "I will fight you." My friend, he—he knows . . . [and] he calls me by "she" and then my first name. It's fine; he's been my friend for so long that it's like, it's normal. But it's like, if someone here who I introduced myself to—I introduced myself as [Mac] and usually most people around here call me "he"; if they call me "she" it's fine; I don't really have a problem with it, but it's like, last year I was going by just "he." . . . But um . . . last year I was, you know, "I'm a he," and there were people that were like "she, she, she, she," and I'm like, "I've never known you before this year, why are you doing this?" But I get, like, yeah, I look outwardly feminine and if you call me a "she" and you don't realize that I'm going by "he," I can understand that. But it's like after I correct you, that's where it gets irritating.

Thus, Mac followed Carter's lead by connecting to Cameron's story and built on it by talking about their name and the use of pronouns.

Ann, who identified as white, still connected with Cameron, albeit in a different way, a way that surprised me. She was responding to what ended up being the last time someone used the word *confusing* to describe Cameron's story. She said, "I mean, I guess like being bigender or gender-fluid or any of those terms that fall under the nonbinary umbrella, that doesn't mean you're necessarily fifty-fifty; you can feel like you're 90 percent a guy and 10 percent a girl, or 80 percent a guy and 10 percent a girl and 10 percent something else." Here, Ann explained to her classmates that being nonbinary does not suggest some even balance between two genders, thus educating them about some gender-fluid people. Then, she went on to connect Cameron's story to her own. She said, "I think there's a difference between—this is coming from some deeply personal stuff; I've been questioning my own gender lately. There's a difference between feeling dysphoric in your gender and dysphoric in your body. Because like, I'm totally cool being a girl, but I don't always feel comfortable in a female body." Beyond this moment, I never, before or after this conversation, heard Ann talk about questioning her gender or sex. Here, though, she named that question as a part of her experience and, further, made the sophisticated move of disentangling gender, that is, "being a girl," from sex, or being "in a female body," as she shared her questions. In these ways, Ann moved toward trans communities.

Just as students connected to Cameron, who we read about and discussed, they connected to one another, like Mac connected to Carter's account of name usage. I also built from the accounts students shared. For example, while Mac was talking about people referring to them using he/him/his, I worried about having used they/them/their. So, I asked:

DR. B.: Okay, so on the first day you said "any pronouns." So, if I—I need to know if you prefer—

MAC: No, no, that [story] was like last year when I was going by just "he."

DR. B.: Okay, because I do not want to be disrespectful to you.

MAC: No, no, you're fine. I did say that was fine. But—

DR. B.: What do you prefer today?

MAC: [*laughs*] I don't care. . . . And don't worry about, because I've had people who [indecipherable] he or she. I'm in the process of questioning again, so don't even worry about it because I feel both ways.

DR. B.: Well, I want you to question as much as you want. But when you land on something, keep me informed, okay?

MAC: Gotcha.

DR. B.: Thank you.

MAC: I am just everywhere. I have a bad habit of just going everywhere when I start talking in this class.

DR. B.: I was following you.

Although I can, in retrospect, see plenty of errors I made in this interaction (like why does Mac have to "land somewhere," at all??), I can also see that I reached out and connected to Mac about something that mattered to them in ways that were respectful even if flawed. I was certainly not alone in striving to be respectful. Katherine explicitly said, "I don't want to be, you know, insulting or disrespectful," and John apologized for first using "he" to refer to Cameron and then started using "they" to talk about Cameron's story.

While reading about Cameron, students moved from feeling confused by to connected with them, thus moving closer to Cameron as a gender-fluid person. For some students, like Carter, this meant moving closer to a gender-fluid community. For others, like Ann, it meant seeing the possibility of entering such communities, and for Mac it meant moving within their gender-fluid community as they came to understand someone who was both alike and unlike them within that community. Like Carter, I moved closer to someone who identified as gender-fluid, but unlike Carter, I did this with a student with whom I shared a class rather than a person about whom I read in a book. This movement around and in gender-fluid communities brought our classroom community closer together, at least in this moment in time, as evidenced by the "deeply personal stuff" people shared within. There was an evolving intimacy as we moved.

Moving around and in Trans Communities

In the second and third semesters of the class, like in the first, students read Kuklin's (2014) *Beyond Magenta*. In these later two classes, though, students selected either Arin Andrews's (2014) *Some Assembly Required: The Not-So-Secret Life of a Transgender Teen* or Katie Rain Hill's (2014) *Rethinking Normal: A Memoir in Transition* to read alongside *Beyond Magenta*. The Andrews and Hill books are autobiographies of trans teens, the two of whom knew and dated each other, so they appear in each other's books.

In an effort to facilitate students talking across the books, I created journal-entry prompts that applied to both books at similar stopping points in them. So, for example, in the section I focus on next, the writing prompt was about chapters 10–12 of both books. It read, "Arin Andrews and Katie Rain Hill describe their early transitions. What do they identify as the key components of their transitions? Why were these so important?" When students in the third-semester class talked about Arin's transition, Abbot, one of two straight and cisgender young men in the class, immediately said "starting testosterone." Next, the only gay man in the class, Khalil, said "therapy sessions." Abbot spoke again, talking about Arin's first day living publicly as a man, and Darren, the other straight and cis man, said just learning that trans people exist. Then Lisa named getting a binder, and I mentioned his getting a packer.

Across these comments, I heard students trying to connect with Arin. Abbot identified a characteristic they share: testosterone. Khalil was a young person who experimented extensively with gender both privately and publicly, both in his daily routine and onstage, during performances. It was quite likely that he knew that were he to transition, it would require therapy sessions. At the time of this conversation, I had not yet learned that Lisa was grappling with her gender identity. By the end of the semester, I knew she was, but she had not asked me to use different names or pronouns. Therefore, it is certainly possible that at the time of this conversation she either had considered wearing or had worn or even was wearing a binder. I cannot know that. What I know is that is what stood out to her as a key component of Arin's transition, and what I suspect is that she was connecting to Arin by naming that aloud in the class. As students reached out to connect with Arin, they moved closer to him and thus closer to trans communities.

When students in the second-semester class talked about the two books after having read them both, some of the cisgender students moved into trans-ally communities, and the only gender-fluid student moved to be in a trans community with Arin—again, just for moments in time. Yanika and Vic, for example, worried that Arin was hurt by Katie not just because she cheated on and broke up with him but also because she said, according to Yanika, "I need a real man!" Vic elaborated on this, saying, "That was kind of rude, and especially since, because I'm sure she might have experienced people not seeing her as a real woman, and that hurts, so it's kind of wrong to, like, say, 'I need a real man.'" Here, Yanika and Vic strove to be trans allies by reflecting on how Arin might experience transphobia, even that expressed by another transgender person, like Katie.

Mac, the only gender-fluid student in the class, took Katie's comment more personally, more passionately. Mac said, "The 'real man' really made me mad, because he is a real man. Like, he doesn't have [indecipherable] genitals, but he is a man, and I figure she would know, like, out of all people, she would know how that would feel. If he was like, 'I need a real woman,' I don't think she'd react to that well. That kind of, like, she said that, I cringed. I'm like, 'Oh no.' He was destroyed; he was described as [indecipherable] destroyed." Mac identified with Arin as a member of a trans community and recognized Katie as a traitor therein. Mac challenged themself to empathize with Katie, saying things like, "I will admit that she has helped him grow; she made him feel a lot safer with, you know, his vulnerabilities and body dysphoria. So that's one thing." Further, they readily admitted their bias for Arin, saying, "Arin's kind of my baby right now; he's kind of my child. . . . I just connect with him really, like, at a deep level." In doing so, Mac further showed their location within a trans community—that is, Arin's—reluctantly acknowledging Katie's position there as well.

In these encounters, students drew on their past and present experiences—for example, with testosterone in the case of Abbot—and even their potential experiences—for example, with therapists in the case of Khalil or binders in the case of Lisa—to move close to trans communities as they engaged with Arin Andrews's story. In doing so, they opened up possible futures for themselves, not that they would necessarily move into, but that they could imagine. Students also asserted positions close to one another in trans-ally communities by calling out the transphobic comment of a trans woman in the book we were reading. Their positionality was affirmed by another student, who did not stand with them in trans-ally communities but in a place of authority on the issue, as they identified as gender-fluid. From this location, Mac acknowledged the tensions within the trans community in they which found themself, at least for the time being.

School and Class Conversations

The school held a panel discussion on issues pertinent to trans people in the fall of 2015, toward the second half of the semester. The event was held in a large, open space, which held half of the student body. I attended the first of two sessions since that's when the seniors attended and all of my students that term were seniors. The audience was facing the panel; to the audience's right was a screen with a Twitter feed. Panelists comprised four students and two guests, all of whom appeared to be white. The principal and school counselor facilitated the event, starting with a rationale for the event. Next, all of the panelists introduced themselves. Both of the guests were doctoral students with whom I had worked, in various capacities, at a nearby university. One identified as a woman and the other identified as a trans man; the latter worked as a part-time counselor in the school. The students from the school included one senior and three sophomores. I later learned that they were volunteers from the school's trans support group. The senior and one of the sophomores used he/him/his pronouns. One of the sophomores used she/her/hers pronouns, and the third sophomore used they/them/their pronouns. The audience applauded energetically after every introduction. Then, the school counselor stated directions for using the Twitter wall, and the principal asked the panel for a definition of *transgender*. The students pointed to the part-time counselor on the panel to answer, and he did; then the other guest distinguished between *transgender* and *transsexual*. The principal asked what words not to use, and both students and guests responded. By the third question, about how it feels to be misgendered, students were taking the lead in responding. There was a question about the meaning of *cisgender* and a question about using they/them/their pronouns. When a question was asked about *queer* and *genderqueer*, the only genderqueer student started to reply but seemed to struggle. The part-time counselor helped and supported what they were saying.

I noticed that the audience was very attentive and quiet throughout. I also noticed that two of my students were sitting in front of me: Mac, who was gender-fluid, and Carter, who was a pansexual cisgender woman. They were clearly engaged, making comments to each other. Mac's leg was on Carter's leg. Carter's hand was in Mac's lap. I had shared class with these two for months and had never noticed their being physically affectionate with each other. I interpreted their actions as supportive, not as romantic. I don't think this panel was easy on Mac, in particular, but I think it meant a lot to them.

The Twitter wall started to come to life with directives and advice, like "Don't treat me like a trans* kid" and "Add 'queerfolk' to 'ladies and gentlemen.'" Then there were questions about how to disclose trans identities, how to ask about pronouns, what about bathrooms, and relationships to sexual identities. These continued after the panel, along with much praise, but panelists responded to some of the questions during the panel, particularly the ones about bathrooms and disclosing to parents. One audience member stood up and said, "Don't call me by my former name." Another audience member asked how people reacted, and one student panelist replied saying she did not even notice people's reactions because she felt so confident in herself. As the principal invited final thoughts from the panelists, the bell rang, but the audience stayed seated until the speakers were done and the audience was excused. Mac and Carter asked me if we could discuss the panel in class the next day, and I agreed.

The next morning, I asked who attended the panel. Just over half had not. Mac said, "Is there any questions that anyone who didn't go to the panel had?" Students wanted to know how it was organized, who spoke, and how people responded. I said, "None of [the responses] felt, like, disruptive or rude," but Mac said their friend was a panelist in the second session and he said that there was a "group of people that were kind of making a joke out of it." A connection was made to the previous year's panel on race, which was discussed at length before I tried to conclude the discussion. Then, one student asked about various pronouns, which we discussed for a bit. Katherine said she was glad that the school was "really good with pronouns," and Mac said that they appreciated that the panelists "touched upon the fact that 'they' is, like, grammatically correct."

The conversation then shifted from the panel to those of us in the room. Hilary wanted to know whether I knew the two panelists from the university and whether I knew they were trans. I explained that they both transitioned before I met them but that they had disclosed to me their trans history, one more privately than the other. Vic said it was easier for her when she met trans people after their transitions because she was less likely to get confused and misgender them. Yanika said she usually did not get people's names wrong but she sometimes got people's pronouns wrong. She said, "I always, like, apologize, but they still get mad at me. Some would say it's all right." She went on to explain, "Whenever, like, I apologize, I always do it, like, in private." In this exchange the students, particularly Vic and Yanika, both of whom identified as cisgender women, moved cautiously but not comfortably near trans people. Mac moved themself near Vic and Yanika, saying, "I find that it's a lot easier to do it, like—so, when my ex first came out to me as trans, it was a lot easier to switch the pronouns to, like, what he wanted over the text. And then when I talked to him, I've accidentally slipped up, and then like, 'I've got to get better.' . . . So I—I kind of understand." Mac moved themself closer to trans people, particularly to their ex, than Vic and Yanika did, but not among them, at least not in this moment in time. All three of them moved themselves to be among trans allies, closer to trans people, as they struggled and strived, made themselves uncomfortable, did the work, apologized, and did more of the work.

Then, though, Mac shifted from telling a story about themself, using "I," to using both "I" and "you." Sometimes when they did this, I understood them to be merging "I" and "you," so, for example, they said, "Because, like, over text you can just delete the message and be like, 'Oh wait, that's not right,' and then fix it. But when you're speaking it just comes out." Here, when Mac used "you," I believe they were speaking to their own experience but allowing for the possibility of other people having experienced something similar. Other times, though, I understood Mac to have used "I" in reference to themself and "you" in reference to Vic, Yanika, and other people learning to be trans allies. For example, Mac said, "And it's like—you slip up; you're human. As long as you know that it was a mistake and that you try, I feel like that's what counts. Like it's still frustrating; that's okay." In doing so, Mac moved themself within and among trans communities but also near an understanding of trans allies. They moved from one to another with only shifts in language.

The panel and our discussion of it invited a broader understanding of trans people. I said, "What I heard on the panel was that [misgendering] hurts," and Mac confirmed, "It does." I recalled how one student panelist said she "didn't want so much attention drawn to it. Like, she wanted—she said it just kind of exacerbated that the hurt came with it." Vic recalled that another student panelist said, "Don't put a big thing around him being trans. Just like—just treat him like a regular [guy] . . . Like don't make it a big deal; don't be like, 'Oh by the way he's trans.'" I explained that the two guests from the university felt quite differently about being recognized as trans. I said, "[She] said, 'I identify as a woman now because I'm done with my transitioning. The transition is complete. I don't identify as a trans woman.' Whereas I think [he] identifies as . . . more comfortably identifies as a man but in conversation *will* identify as [a] trans man." Thus, we talked about some of the gender diversity within trans communities. Mac added to our understanding of the diversity of trans communities in this interaction, toward the end of the conversation:

YANIKA: So was [the panel], like, beneficial? Was it, like, good?

MAC: I—I feel like it was. I was really worried they wouldn't bring up gender-fluid.

DR. B.: There was a lot of talk with fluidity.

MAC: I was really worried that they wouldn't do it.

DR. B.: Yeah, but they did.

MAC: I was happy about it.

Whereas Vic, Yanika, and I moved ourselves toward and among trans-ally communities as we came to understand some of the complexity of trans communities, Mac moved themself toward and within trans communities, thus contributing to their diversity. These movements drew upon our past and present experiences, but they also projected toward a future in which we could exist in and among trans-ally and trans communities with a knowledge of and respect for diversity among them.

Masculine Men

Not everyone was moving toward trans-ally and trans communities, though. Consider John, for example. John was a white, cisgender, straight young man. Very early in our course, I assigned the "Heteronormativity Scavenger Hunt" as homework. (This activity was shared by Summer Pennell. For more about it, read Blackburn & Pennell, 2018.) Everyone did the homework, and almost everyone completed it. For this assignment, John identified gender-defined bathrooms as an example of heteronormativity, and he identified "unisex bathrooms" as a potential disruption. He acknowledged gender-defined bathrooms as existing in schools and that they might make queer people "uncomfortable." But when it came to the final question—"What can you do to make these places more friendly [for queer people]?"—he did not answer. I wrote, "Think on this one, [John]. It's the whole point of the assignment. Push yourself." He wasn't moving.

Shortly thereafter, the class talked about how Walt Whitman's "America" failed to include women in any substantial way. So, when the students created their own version of the poem, most people used they/them/their pronouns and other words to avoid gendering their contributions. Only two people gendered their contributions as from men (and none as from women). One of those two people was John. Later, when there was a school panel on issues pertinent to trans people, John was at school but elected not to attend the panel. I saw him sitting outside of the school, under a tree. The next day, when we discussed the panel, even when Mac explicitly asked whether people who were not present had any questions, John said nothing. In these ways, I saw John remaining quite distant from trans people and trans allies.

Not only did John distance himself from trans people and trans allies, he stood firmly as a masculine man. This was evident when I asked students to brainstorm two lists of characteristics—one for how men are described in the United States and another for how women are. Here, I was again working with an activity I had recently been taught by Summer Pennell (for more on this, read Blackburn & Pennell, 2018). I led this activity at the start of a unit on memoir, in which we would read *Beyond Magenta* as a class and either *Rethinking Normal* or *Some Assembly Required* independently, because these texts disrupt gender in various ways. The activity was in this way aligned. To start the activity, I typed the lists as they offered ideas (see table 1).

Once they developed the lists, I instructed students to stand all the way toward one end of the room or the other if "all of those things, every single one of those descriptions . . . hold true for you." I explained, "If it's somewhere in between, you decide where. Stand somewhere in between." Students moved between the two points, and I asked them why they stood where they stood. Most students stood "somewhere in between" and explained how they exhibited some characteristics from one list and others from the other. Some of the characteristics were on both lists as opposites. For example, Mac said, "I do feel like I have to protect people, but it's like a mutual thing, where I protect you and you protect me."

John, however, stood out in that he stood all the way over to the "men" side. I said, "John, you are so far over you're almost beyond," and then proceeded to ask him about most of the items on the list:

DR. B.: So, you don't think you should cry or be emotional?

JOHN: No.

Table 1. Chart created in the fall 2015 class to characterize traits typically associated with men and women

How Men Are Described in Our Society	How Women Are Described in Our Society
Shouldn't cry or be emotional	Need to be protected
Protectors of women	Really emotional, moody
Big, strong, weight lifting	Delicate, dainty
Leaders	Not physically strong
Not as clean, don't care about physical appearance as much	Dream of the long white dress, tiered cake, wedding
Pay for dates	Child responsibilities
Propose marriage, initiate dates	Helpers

DR. B.: Really?

JOHN: I almost never cry. It's been about three years.

DR. B.: Aww. Okay, do you feel like you need to protect women?

JOHN: Yeah.

DR. B.: Do you weight lift? Lift weights?

JOHN: Yeah.

DR. B.: You don't care about your physical appearance?

JOHN: Not at all.

[*laughter*]

DR. B.: You pay for dates?

JOHN: Yeah.

DR. B.: You initiate dates?

JOHN: Mhm.

DR. B.: All right. Then you get to stand all the way over there.

He fully claimed everything generated on the list of descriptors of men. And despite multiple invitations to switch locations, offered to the class as a whole, John never moved.

I was so struck by his rejection of anything beyond the masculine that I spoke directly to him as I transitioned the class from the gender-line activity to a discussion of the early chapters in the Hill and Andrews books. I said, "I'm hoping that, um, by—it will be interesting, [John], to see how it will play out for you. Um, but I'm hoping that by playing with these ideas some, that you will be able to identify with characters we're reading about and kind of reflect on your own way of being, um, in between or not, and how it connects with the characters." I knew that I would be asking students to move between their current gendered communities and those of the people we would be reading about and discussing. I could see the potential in most students to move within and among gendered communities, but I could not see it in John. I saw a rigidity, perhaps even a defensiveness. John seemed to stand firmly as a masculine man.

This is not to stay that a masculine identity is not a viable one, for a man or anyone else. It certainly is. Regrettably, I seemed to dismiss that possibility in my reactions to John during this activity. I believe I was worried that a man who clung so fervently to his masculinity would not identify with trans characters like Katie Rain Hill and Arin Andrews and, much more importantly, would not move toward trans-ally communities. And, in fact, I saw no evidence of such movement in this student, no push, no pull, just a digging in of the heels, of his heels.

Not only did I see no movement in the present discussion of gender, I saw no evidence of a history of movement of John having gotten to this place in terms of gender, and, just as importantly, I saw no indication of any potential movement in terms of gender. In fact, Ahmed talks about needing to be able to see where one might go next in order to move to get there, but even being about to see something new requires some sort of movement, and here I saw none at all. These are the stances I experience as unethical.

Ethical Movement with Respect to Gender Diversity in Classroom Encounters

Although not all students moved toward trans-ally and trans communities, many of them did, at least in some moments in time. As they discussed fiction and nonfiction literature and students' lives, including but not limited to their own, students moved around and in trans-ally and trans communities, including gender-fluid communities. They showed agility. At times, when they encountered peers or characters unlike themselves, they kept distant, deciphering instead of empathizing. This could have resulted in a sort of ossification. But when they moved closer, something gave in those encounters. The movement was fraught with struggle, but when it happened it was movement with consequence, where students came to understand one another and themselves with more complexity and nuance. They connected. Again, they exhibited some agility. This makes an encounter ethical. Not that it was easy or comfortable, but that it was work, and that it mattered.

Chapter 3

Moving with Respect to
Racial Diversity in Classroom Encounters

The United States was founded on racist ideas and behaviors, and these ideas and behaviors, while morphing, have existed throughout our history, including during the time of this study (Kendi, 2016). Also, throughout US history, including during the time of this study, there have been antiracist ideas and behaviors. During the time of this study, there was a resurgence of people and organizations who were invested in the fallacy of white supremacy, on the one hand. The massacre at the Emanuel African Methodist Episcopal Church in Charleston, South Carolina, happened in June of 2015. The Unite the Right rally in Charlottesville, Virginia, was in August of 2017. On the other hand, as I mention in the introduction, the Black Lives Matter movement was gaining significant national attention. The protests in Ferguson had started, and, as the elections were gearing up, Black Lives Matter was playing a role. Racial tensions were (and are) high. In order to explore how the high school students in my LGBTQ+-themed literature courses used language, including written language, to move in terms of racist behaviors, I rely on particular understandings of race, racism, and antiracism, which I describe next.

Race, in and of itself, is a "social construction and not a fixed, static category rooted in some notion of innate biological differences" (Omi & Winant, 2014, p. 12). It is "neither stable nor consistent" (Omi & Winant, 2014, p. 2). According to Omi and Winant (2014), it is "being made and remade from moment to moment" (p. 264), and, as such, "it varies according to time and place" (p. 13). Still, race is a social construct of great consequence. "Race creates new forms of power: the power to categorize and judge, elevate and downgrade, include and exclude" (Kendi, 2019, p. 38). In Kendi's (2019) words, "Race is a mirage but one that we do well to see, while never forgetting it is a mirage, never forgetting that it's the powerful light of racist power that makes the mirage" (p. 37).

Racism in the United States has been "shaped by a centuries-long conflict between white domination and resistance by people of color" (Omi & Winant, 2014, p. 3), and while racism is "institutional, structural, and systemic" (Kendi, 2019, p. 18), Kendi argues that *racist* (and *antiracist*) are labels better used to describe ideas and behaviors rather than a person or groups of people. A racist idea, he says, is "any idea that suggests one racial group is inferior or superior to another racial group in any way" (Kendi, 2019, p. 20). In contrast, an antiracist idea is "any idea that suggests the racial groups are equals in all their apparent differences—that there is nothing right or wrong with any racial group" (Kendi, 2019, p. 20). Omi and Winant (2014) also talk about antiracist projects as "those that *undo or resist structures of domination based on racial significations and identities*" (p. 129). That said, *racist* (and *antiracist*) can be used as labels to describe people if they are used "like peelable name tags that are placed and replaced based on what someone is doing or not doing, supporting or expressing in each moment. These are not permanent tattoos" (Kendi, 2019, p. 23). Some people's ideas and behaviors are relatively consistent over periods of time, creating the illusion of a tattoo, but it is an illusion, and, again, an illusion of consequence.

Antiracist projects are imperative. That they are essential for people of color is obvious, but they are also necessary for white people, or, as Coates (2015) asserts, people who imagine themselves to be white. According to Kendi (2019), "As long as the mind is racist, the mind can never be free" (p. 105). He further argues that even though "ordinary White people benefit from racist policies," white people would benefit more from an "equitable society" (p. 129). Therefore, becoming antiracist is the "basic struggle we're all in, the struggle to be fully human and to see that others are fully human" (Kendi, 2019, p. 11). The question then is, How do we become antiracist? Kendi (2019) says, "We know how to be racist. We know how to pretend to be not racist. Now let's learn how to be antiracist" (p. 11). It is, however, one of those things that we must learn and relearn again and again. We cannot *be* antiracist, statically, but we can *become* antiracist, in perpetuity, with "persistent self-awareness, constant self-criticism, and regular self-examination" (Kendi, 2019, p. 23).

Racist and antiracist behaviors, ideas, and projects have the effect of moving people in relation to one another. They can move people closer to people whom they respect and honor (and who respect and honor them in return) and farther away from those whom they do not (and, again, vice versa). In this chapter, I focus on white, Black, and Mexican American people and communities, knowing that these communities are multiple and variable, they are complicated and messy, and they are only a few among infinite others. I focus on them knowing that they are not only racialized communities but also national and ethnic communities among many other kinds of communities, but I focus on them here anyway because the students did in our conversations about race. I examine how students used language, including written language, to move closer to and farther from racist ideas and behaviors to reflect on the consequences of such movement in schools and classrooms.

More specifically, I start by looking at how white people pushed Black people out of classroom and school communities, effectively racializing those communities in ways that are aligned with the fallacy of white supremacy. I then consider how Black people pulled themselves into the embrace of Black communities to protect themselves against racist ideas and behaviors. I then look beyond Black and white communities and focus on Mexican American communities. Next, I explore how students discussed the differences, tensions, and power dynamics within their own racialized communities before finally examining the ways that some students who imagined themselves to be white (Coates, 2015) struggled to remove the "peelable name tags," in Kendi's (2019) words, of "racist" and to earn the right to wear the ones of "antiracist," sometimes with the encouragement of others wearing "antiracist" name tags in particular moments in time.

White People Pushing Black People Out

White people pushed themselves away from racially diverse communities and reified their immersion in white communities—even communities invested in the fallacy of white supremacy—by refusing to engage in conversations about race and racism or refusing to do so in ways that implicated them in racist dynamics. That is, they refused to use and examine their own language around race and racism. An explicit example of this is from when the first group of students, most of whom were white and only one of whom was biracial Asian and white, were discussing *Brooklyn, Burning* (Brezenoff, 2011), a novel in which neither the main character nor the love interest is identifiable in terms of gender. I asked, "Are the characters raced, in your mind?" Two students said "no," then another, who was white and queer, said, "God. Quit. Don't do that. We haven't even figured out what gender they are." Thus, this student moved actively to shut down the conversation about race (Schey & Blackburn, 2019b).

Other times, the effort was more subtle. In the second-semester class, which was more racially diverse, we were discussing *Aristotle and Dante Discover the Secrets of the Universe* (Sáenz, 2012) and focusing on a journal prompt asking the students to consider what Ari and Dante considered to be "Mexican," including why Dante did not feel Mexican enough. After some conversation, John made a move to locate the novel historically. Even though the novel is set in the late 1980s, John connected it to the late 1960s and early 1970s and the "iconic hippy." He said, "They didn't really judge people based on race at all. But they're one of the only generations that can honestly say, 'I don't judge people by race.' Because I feel even people who [say they] don't do [that] now, subconsciously do." I understood his "they" to refer back to his use of "iconic hipp[ies]," indexing a particular kind of white person. Further, I understood John as praising these white people for not "judg[ing] people by race," but, to push this a bit further, I heard him as praising white people for being color-blind, a term and concept I assumed was unfamiliar to him and therefore did not use in our conversation. Still, John evaded talking about race himself by lauding white people who claim color-blindness, as if to say, "If I cannot see race, then there is nothing to talk about." In these ways, some white students sometimes strove to make themselves more comfortable in whiteness and, in doing so, erased people of color by refusing to see them. It was a metaphorical genocide. Here, John located himself solidly among white people, and, more specifically, not the color-blind white people of the hippy generation but contemporary white people who "judge people based on race." He did not move there; he was already there. By staying there, he effectively shut down the possibility of future antiracist encounters.

One way that white people push themselves away from Black people, in particular, is by imagining them as angry or upset (Ahmed, 2010, 2014). Whether this is a conscious act is irrelevant, because either way it is an act of consequence, a racist behavior. By imagining some Black people as angry or upset, some white people feel entitled to push them away, refuse to engage with them, or dismiss what they are saying. I should also say that I am not dismissing the value of anger. Many times, people, particularly people of color, have good reason to be angry in our racist society. And, as Ahmed (2012) says, "Anger could open up the world" (p. 171). What I am talking about here, though, is different; it is when (white) people misinterpret Black people as angry as a result of their racist expectations.

This happened, albeit discreetly, in one of our class discussions. We had just read Huey P. Newton's 1970 speech to the Black Panthers entitled "The Women's Liberation and Gay Liberation Movements" (BlackPast, 2018), a text suggested to me by Lance McCready. Desiree, who identified as "Black and proud," was the first to speak up to discuss the text. She quoted part of the text, saying, " 'I have hang-ups [myself] about male homosexuality' and not female sexuality." She said that this was "still relevant today." Another student took up Desiree's comment, saying, "I'm glad you brought that up," and extended Desiree's point. Then Abbot, one of two white, straight, cisgender young men in the class, tried to explain why Newton may have "hang-ups about male homosexuality." He said, "Well, I mean, to a certain extent, it does make sense, because I'm assuming they're mostly talking about straight men who think that way, and if you think about it, he's not into men. So, if it's two females, it's just two of what he's into, so it would be easy to understand why." He went on to consider the issue from alternative perspectives: "But at the same time, it's like—it would be okay if you felt that way but just didn't have a problem with male homosexuality but didn't engage in it. But a lot of these people truly have no problem with female homosexuality but actually have bias toward male homosexuality. And it really doesn't make sense. It kind of makes it seem like they're barbarian or something." Abbot was, it seems to me, grappling not only with Newton's stance but also his own, particularly when he used "you." When he switched to "these people," though, he seemed to separate himself from men who are homophobic against other men but not women, men he considered to be "barbarian."

At this point, Desiree had an immediate reaction that is neither visible nor audible on the video recording of the class but that I noted verbally: "You had a reaction to that. What were you going to say?" And she quickly said, "No. Never mind." Then Kristy, a white young woman in the class, responded almost immediately, "I think, like, in a nicer way what Abbot is trying to say is like—." Whether or not Kristy was defending Abbot from Desiree is impossible to tell, but that Desiree understood her in this way was evident by the fact that she interrupted what Kristy was saying to explain, "Oh, I wasn't upset," at which time Kristy spoke over Desiree, who was still speaking, to say, "No, I know what you're saying," which seemed all but impossible since Desiree had not said it. She had elected not to. Desiree continued to explain, "It was like, he was saying something, I was going to say something, but then he finished his sentence, so then I didn't have to say something." Here, Desiree clearly understood Kristy as having perceived her as upset and clarified that this was a misperception. Kristy effectively pushed Desiree away from her, even pushed her out of the conversation, moving herself into a conversation with Abbot, another white person. In this way, Kristy constructed the class, at this moment in time, as an anti-Black one. This encounter, then, was one that only opened up possibilities of racist encounters and closed down possibilities of antiracist ones.

Such racist behaviors happened school-wide, as well. The school held a series of panels to discuss race. There were three panels during my time at the school, one in 2015 and two in 2016, with the third being a follow-up to the second. The day after the second race-themed panel, in February of 2016, school started slowly because there had been an ice storm overnight. As students trickled into my room, I asked about the previous day's panel. When I initiated the topic, there were just two seniors in the room, a young Black woman named Jenna and a young white man named Darren. They told me about the format, how it started with student performances and followed with a student panel answering only a few questions read by two teachers. Jenna listed the students on the panel, all of whom were Black, although not all African American. No one described the audience, but it was likely as racially diverse as the school's student body, the majority of which (about 56 percent) was white.

Darren said the questions included "Why isn't there a white history month?" and "Should we be treated equally or specially . . . based on [our] culture?" He described the questions as "honest . . . like if you could ask a Black person a question now, what would you ask?" In saying this, the assumed "you" is not only a white person but a white person who has done very little work to reflect on their racism. Jenna didn't speak to the questions except to say she could not recall the third. When I asked whether the panelists seemed to be under attack, both Darren and Jenna said they were fine. However, Darren reported that "a lot of students [in the audience] did not respond well to [the panelists' answers]. They felt like they were being attacked." Later, in an interview with me, Delilah, who identified as Mexican American, described this panel as "terrible."

She said that the panel had no diversity in that it comprised only Black students and that the audience was understood as white, not because it only included white people, which was not the case, but because that was whom the speakers addressed. She said,

> It was more or less pointing fingers, and, like, "Oh, you did this to me." And blah blah blah. And I'm just sitting here like, "None of us are slaves." . . . Like, come on. Like, none of us are in shackles, getting our teeth checked. Calm down. Like, this is not about who did what. This is more or less to enlighten what happened in the history and how far we've come. Like, not about "You did this," and, like, "No." . . . Like, it was, it was bad. The whole school unraveled. And you could really tell the true colors. And it was like, being Hispanic, um, I'm kind of glad that I was. . . . Because, like, you could obviously see the division. Like— . . . the white kids, and the Black kids, and they just [*mouth noise*]. . . . And the people who are in the middle, like Asians, Hispanics, and everything else—they were just kind of like, "Eh, you guys are both crazy." . . . "Can you guys stop?" . . . It was more or less like, we could just see the whole division.

When she said "none of *us* are slaves . . . none of *us* are in shackles, getting our teeth checked," she moved herself to be with Black people, specifically African American people and their history of being enslaved by white people in the United States. However, she also moved above the Black panelists, as if she had authority over them, telling them to "calm down" and telling them what the panel was and was not about. Then she moved herself "in the middle" as a "Hispanic" person with Asian Americans "and everything else." From this location, she saw both Black students and white students as "crazy," implying her location was that of the uniquely sane. That she experienced this panel intensely is made obvious by her saying that the "whole school unraveled" in response to it.

Eventually, though, Delilah went on to move herself closer to white people, and, as such, she reported feeling threatened by Black people. She said, "Because [in] the first panel I was ignoring everything. . . . Because I even felt threated. I was like 'Whoah.' Like, because my color, like I'm white obviously, like skin color. . . . But ethnicity-wise I'm not. So, it's, I even felt threatened. I was like 'Whoah, I'm white too, but I'm kind of yellow. So I don't know.' . . . I felt really threatened." Muñoz (2000) says, "The effect of Latinos/as is often off. One can even argue that it is off-white" (p. 70). This is how I understand Delilah to be describing herself when she refers to her white-yellow skin in relationship to feeling threatened by the Black panelists—as an "off-white" person, she felt threatened by Black panelists and therefore ignored what they had to say. She used her feelings as a reason for making racist comments and ignoring Black voices. Darren supported such feelings and actions by normalizing the questions and representing the panelists as attacking. These students pushed themselves away from Black communities and pulled themselves toward racist ones.

Let me be clear that none of these students were students I would have "tattooed," to use Kendi's language, as racist. But these were classroom encounters, moments in time, when racist ideas were evident, even if only upon analysis. And I share responsibility for these encounters. I was the teacher in them, and there was not some super antiracist intervention that I just excluded here to make a point. I pushed back some on John but not on the students in the other conversations. I felt some unease in those moments, but it was only upon analysis that I came to understand why. My understanding was developed through careful deliberation, which, for me, is slow at first. I get better and faster at it with practice, but at first it is slow. And opportunities were thus lost; opportunities for antiracist future encounters were prevented. And some Black students did not have time for this nonsense.

Black People Pulling Themselves into the Embrace of Black Communities

As I mentioned, Desiree identified as "Black and proud." Her great-grandmother frequently told her the story of when she was Desiree's age, seventeen, and "marched with Martin Luther King" on Washington. Moreover, Desiree actively sought and fostered relationships with other Black people who helped to raise her up. She said about Tumblr,

> If you follow the right people and interact with the right peo-
> ple—like I have a lot of friends that are states away because
> they made a group chat for people who were Black and on
> Tumblr and I ended up joining it about a year ago. And some
> of these people are my best friends. Like I don't, like I still talk

to them every day. Like every single day, like, we talk every single day, and they're there for me when I need them, and I'm there for them when they need me. Like, we have each other's number; we Facetime; I talk to these people all the time. So, Tumblr is like a safe place for me in a way. . . . And, like, they talk about things other than just being Black. They talk about suicide awareness, trans awareness, and things like that. . . . So, like, if you follow the right people, you get a positive reaction from stuff like Tumblr. And I love it. And they have this thing called Blackout, and it happens, I think, once a month. And, where you just post selfies of you, and it's like and everyone reblogs it and everyone likes it. It's because you're, it's because Black people don't get recognized for being beautiful who they are. . . . So we take a day on Tumblr. Or we'll take a day on any, it's every social media, and we do it to represent ourselves.

In these ways, Desiree fed her racial pride so that she could survive and thrive (Love, 2019) in our racist society. Of course, she brought these experiences into the race-themed panels, where she was in the audience.

Desiree was not offended by the panelists; indeed, she supported them, but she was, understandably, offended by the question posed about "white history month." In an interview, she praised one of the panelist's responses to that question. According to her, the panelist answered, "There is a white history month. . . . There is eleven months dedicated to [white people] and even this month [February], because people take it away from Black people because they want to know why, why isn't this a month for other races." Desiree reflected on this interaction. She said,

> That [question] completely pissed me off because, one, I've sat in school my whole entire life, and I've learned about you guys' history, and on top of that we don't learn about the negative things white people have done . . . except for slavery, and then every year in February we talk about the same Black, we talk about . . . um . . . Dr. Martin Luther King, maybe Malcolm X, Harriet Tubman, like, we talk about the same, I've learned about the same people my whole entire life. If I didn't research anybody else, I would not know. . . . When do you learn about our history? Like, the month is to learn about our history, and you guys still take that away from us.

Desiree thus captured tensions between Black and white communities, noting how Black people have to learn about white people all of the time whereas white people complain of just a single month of learning about the same Black people over and over again. In supporting the Black panelists, explicitly naming a few prominent Black people in US history, and talking about the importance of knowing about more than just these few, Desiree pushed away from ideas and behaviors associated with the fallacy of white supremacy and pulled herself into the embrace of Black communities. In doing so, she opened up possibilities of future antiracist encounters and a future of Black joy.

In an interview, Jenna and Khalil explained that it was the response to the panel that offended them rather than the question itself, as with Desiree, or the panelist's answer, as with Delilah. Jenna, who identified as Black, could acknowledge Delilah's experiences but could also recognize that Delilah's were not universal. Jenna said, "Some people did [feel attacked], some people enjoyed [the panel], some people didn't like it." From her point of view, she could see that some people enjoyed it and even those who didn't enjoy it did not necessarily feel like Delilah felt. But, again, for Jenna and Khalil it was the response that drew their attention. Jenna said the panel "started off a lot of wars from the school." And Khalil continued, "Yeah, it was Facebook, Twitter, Instagram, Snapchat. It was just war all around the school." That they used the word "war" indicates that the response felt intense if not violent. They were particularly struck by a "white girl," in Khalil's words, who was, according to him, "friends with a lot of Black people." She was pushing the issue of whether there should be a Black History Month:

> KHALIL: This one [white] girl. She went on Facebook and was like, "So you guys [Black people] are mad because you guys get 29, 28, 29 days of a year. Wow." . . . And she was like, "But we [white people] don't get any." And I was like—
>
> DR. BLACKBURN: Every stupid day.
>
> KHALIL: Yeah. And she was like, "Well, what about in October, November, you know, the LGBT month; in April it's autism."

He went on to say what he would have liked to have said to her when he saw her in the halls but he would not because he did not want to get in trouble at school. He would insult her, saying, "You're not even cute," but he would also educate her about the accomplishments of Black people, saying,

> KHALIL: First off, there are Black people who made the stop-light, the toilets, all this stuff, even peanut butter, and you eat peanut butter but you're still, like, criticizing us. The bars in your face from your piercings, I'm pretty sure somebody had to help with that. I mean, you go to Africa, you actually see people with stuff in their face, so you're pretty much—

> DR. B.: Mirroring African tradition.

> KHALIL: Yeah. [Shayla, a Black person who was on staff at the school] said when Kylie Jenner decided to put cornrows in her hair . . . But, you know, we do it, we're known as thugs and all that. But she can go out there and do whatever she wants. . . . So, seeing her, I just want to tell her about herself, like . . . like "everything that you want, I already have."

Khalil pushed the "white girl" who was "friends with a lot of Black people" away from Black communities by criticizing and ignoring her. This push was to keep her away from Black people so as to keep them safe from her racist behaviors. Khalil also pointed to tensions between Black and white people in saying how white people can do what Black people are criticized for with no negative consequences. But also, importantly, he pulled himself in with African Americans and Africans asserting pride in their accomplishments and contributions. Thus, both Khalil and Desiree, at this moment in time, pulled themselves into Black communities, refusing to accommodate the racist behaviors of white people.

Here, Desiree, Jenna, and Khalil moved toward Black communities and stood there. Their stances were like those we saw in the first chapter, when Parker, Sherry, and Simon, all of whom identified as queer and white, worked hard to move away from the hate they experienced in the homophobic and transphobic world to stand strong among those who embraced them for who they were in terms of their sexual and gender identities. They are not the same; stances defined by sexuality and gender are not the same as those defined by race, but these specific stances are similar in that they are preceded by movement and they hold the potential of movement toward future liberatory encounters.

Beyond Black and White Communities

Racism is, of course, not restricted to between white and Black communities. In fact, when Jenna reflected on the 2015 race-themed panel, she troubled this assumption:

> JENNA: I know there are some students here that are, like, Hispanic, and like—it was somebody else, I forget what race they are—
>
> DR. B.: Racial minorities that aren't African American.
>
> JENNA: Yeah. Like they felt like they were just talking about only, like, African Americans, and like they should at least have included, like, our race into it as well. . . . That's why some people felt a little disappointed.

As a young Black woman, Jenna made space for the critique that other racial minorities were not represented in the 2015 panel, which comprised more than a handful of people. Some students' advisory classes took up where the panel left off in this regard. Right after that panel, Darby, who identified as white, talked about how the conversation in her advisory class went. She said,

> We had a lot of different input, like, about that and about like being not just Black or white, like, we had kids that were talking about like, you know, like a kid named [Anou], he's from Laos. . . . And people that aren't from like—the people that are from different countries are like Asian and stuff like that—they even touched on like how the difference between them actually does matter, and that was really cool to hear people talk about it that weren't like—it was cool to get a different perspective other than just, like, Black and white.

I heard no mention of advisory discussions after the race-themed panels that followed and saw no evidence of increased racial diversity in them.

After the first 2016 panel, Jenna offered the same critique about racial diversity and said that others in the audience had said, "At least [they] could have mentioned other races than just, you know, theirs and their own opinion." Darren suggested that the organizers tried, unsuccessfully, to diversify the panel, which comprised only Black students.

The next race-themed panel at the school was about a month later, and Delilah, who is Mexican American, characterized it at first as "great" and then later, in an interview, as "pretty good." She then shared the following:

DELILAH: We're doing another panel at the end of this month of [inaudible]. Any—well, basically anybody really, they're having another—no, like, I mean, um.

DR. B.: So, broadening the discussion from Black and white to the other ethnicities. Okay, well, excellent. Let me know.

Unfortunately, this panel still had not happened by the end of the year. Delilah did, however, reference a panel that had already happened, one I had not heard of before. She said, "Me and [Nancy] were on the panel for the Latino side, and then some other people on the panel like [Adam] I think." At first, I thought one of the two of us was just confusing tense, but then Kristy said, "I heard your guys's stories." Then, Delilah jumped ahead in time to the expected panel, the one that never happened, and said, "I don't know, I'll probably cry. You don't want to know my stories." Here, she picked up on the talk about Shayla's stories, which I discuss more later in this chapter. Delilah acknowledged the power of Shayla's stories and underscored the power of her own, saying she would cry and that they don't even "want to know" her stories. But then, later in the semester, she asserted that the story of her family is "a story that needs to be told" and that she would be willing to come back even after she graduated to tell it. Delilah thus drew on her past encounters, growing up as a Mexican American in the United States, and she opened up the possibility of future antiracist encounters, offering to serve as a panelist at the school even after she graduated.

Jenna, Darby, and Delilah pushed themselves into racially diverse communities as they engaged in conversations about race that pushed beyond the Black-white dichotomy. Further, Delilah pulled others along with her. As a result of this pushing and pulling, there was movement.

Differences, Tensions, and Power Dynamics
within Mexican American Communities

Just as differences and tensions, pushes and pulls, are not restricted to between white and Black communities, they are not limited to the spaces between particular racialized communities. In other words, these power dynamics exist within communities as well as between or among them.

In class we explored Mexican American communities in our reading and discussion of *Aristotle and Dante Discover the Secrets of the Universe* (Sáenz, 2012). I recognize that to be Mexican is to be associated with a nation and that many races of people are associated with the nation of Mexico. But I also recognize that, as Omi and Winant (2014) state, "the ideas of race and nation [are] deeply connected" (p. 78). In this novel, being Mexican is more about cultural practices than citizenship in one country or another. So, I might instead talk about ethnicity. Darby, for example, said this about the novel: "The difference between how Ari and Dante, even though they're [both] Mexican, is that [the book] like shows the difference . . . you think about ethnicity from the perspective of two people of the same ethnicity, which is really cool. Because I think that like Ari embraces his Mexican culture while Dante like rejects the Mexican stereotypes because he doesn't fit into [the culture]." Similarly, Vic distinguished Ari and Dante's feelings and thoughts about being Mexican in a journal entry in which she wrote, "[Dante] doesn't feel all that 'Mexican' like Ari does" and followed this observation with a quotation from the book, in which Dante tells Ari, " 'I think Mexicans don't like me.' " Thus, this book provoked conversations about who counts as Mexican, who is Mexican enough, and how they, both the characters and the students, know. So, while I could focus on ethnicity here, I am reminded of Omi and Winant's (2014) assertion that "being 'ethnic' turns out to be about whether and how much an individual or group can assimilate into or hybridize with whiteness" (p. 46). Further, Kendi (2019) states, "The fact is, all ethnic groups, once they fall under the gaze and power of race makers, become racialized" (p. 62). Such is the case with Mexicans in the United States now and in our conversations about *Aristotle and Dante*.

In these discussions, there was some awkwardness in terms of the potential of reifying stereotypes, which was appropriate considering the dearth of people able and willing to speak from their own experiences as Mexican Americans. In the first class, there was one white student who had previously lived in the southwestern United States in a predominantly "Hispanic" neighborhood. In the second class, there was one biracial student whose brother lived in a similar community. But the only Mexican American student who took the class did so in the semester where we ran out of time and could not read *Aristotle and Dante* at all. (I continue to be disappointed about this.) The awkwardness, in terms of the potential of reifying stereotypes, was evident when I assigned this writing prompt: "Ari and Dante talk a lot about what it means to be (or not be) Mexican. Point to places in the novel that give you insight into what it means to (not) be Mexican, according to them." Yanika began sharing her entry with "Okay, um, I was really kind of nervous," and I understood her nervousness as about being biracial, Black and white, talking about Mexican characters, and not wanting to stereotype them. In her journal, she said that the quotations she identified were from Dante's perspective and they showed "how the stereotypes influenced his life." She did not share this in the class discussion, though; instead she went on to reference one of the two quotations she selected. This one was from the part of the book where Ari jokingly tells Dante not to steal his truck and Dante responds, continuing the joke, "I'm Mexican. . . . I know all about hotwiring" (Sáenz, 2012, p. 279). This is something one Mexican American character can say to another in a jocular manner, particularly when both were created by a Mexican American author, but not something Yanika would say about them. Stephanie, the only biracial (Asian and white) student in the first class, talked about the same part of the book: "It seems like in the book the people in the younger generation, like Ari and Dante, [have] very like negative stereotype of Mexicans. Like where it says Mexicans hotwire your car and do all these really bad things 'cause they're Mexican." She did not recognize the humor between the boys and made clear that what she understood as their stereotypes were theirs and not her own.

Yanika talked about the importance of names and pointed us to the part of the book where Dante is generating a list of names for his expected baby brother. Dante lists Diego, Joaquin, Rafael, Maximiliano, and Ari says, " 'Those names sound pretty Mexican,' " and Dante responds, " 'Yeah, well, I'm shying away from ancient classical names. And besides, if he has a Mexican name, then maybe he'll *feel* more Mexican' " (Sáenz, 2012, p. 269). Yanika explained, "Choosing those names was a way for Dante to kind of like protect his baby brother and like shield him from feeling the way that Dante feels, like he's, like, not a good Mexican." But, in addition to names, there were nicknames that Ari just knew and accepted but Dante had to decipher, which pointed to the issue of language more broadly. Yanika initiated this discussion:

YANIKA: Well, can Dante speak Spanish? Wasn't there something about, like . . . ?

MAC: He said he couldn't do it well.

YANIKA: What was he talking about when he was? I think that might be part of it.

DR. B.: Definitely.

YANIKA: Just not, not understanding or being able to, like, speak it, [inaudible] and use English.

DR. B.: Right. Yeah! Oh, no, I think the language was a huge part about it.

Names are parts of the larger linguistic practices that Dante feels make some people, like Ari, Mexican and others, like him, not Mexican enough.

Other cultural practices that do this sort of work are related to how people are raised and educated. In the spring 2015 class, for example, Kimberly, who identified as white, said, "I think also, like, how Ari's mom was raised influences how Ari thinks about [being Mexican] a lot because Ari's mom, like, really had to fight against all these stereotypes, and she said something like, 'I'm educated; does that un-Mexicanize me?'" In this part of the novel, Ari's mom tries to teach Ari that schooling is not owned by one nationality or another. Kimberly pointed to this section to show how explicitly Ari's mom talks about being Mexican in ways that debunk stereotypes.

Yanika also tried to debunk stereotypes about being Mexican, but with particular respect to sexuality:

YANIKA: So, we're talking a lot about—or at least I did—[inaudible] Dante, so I was wondering, like, if we learned that Dante likes boys—?

DR. B.: Yes, yes! Good point.

YANIKA: So, I was just wondering, like, does this play into—does that play into, like, being Mexican. Is there, like, a stereotype of, like, Mexicans aren't gay, or something?

DR. B.: That's exactly right. That's exactly right. That is exactly right. So it's [inaudible] machismo, and it's the idea that men are men, right? So that there's no—that means desiring women, it means being tough, it means being stoic, you know, like, keeping your emotions hidden, and so that machismo thing is absolutely a part of, um, some Mexican cultures. I'm not trying to stereotype them by saying that is the—that is a value.

CARTER: Being macho?

DR. B.: Yeah, yeah, it matters. It matters.

MAC: Didn't Dante question that, like, when he was excluding Ari on the trip, he was like—they were talking about what they wanted to eat, and he's like, "Oh, I want to get menudo," and he was like, "Yeah, well I guess you're a real Mexican." And he's like, "A real Mexican likes to kiss boys?" and Ari's like, "I don't think that's an American invention."

YANIKA: Right. I forgot about that.

Please know, I am not and was not saying that Mexican culture is inherently *machista*, rather that machismo emerged as a theme in the text that students explored dynamically. Here the class both acknowledged the stereotype that being gay is not a Mexican thing and is a thing in the United States and disrupted that stereotype by drawing on the language of a character in the book.

Carter, who identified as Black, pushed the disruption further. She wondered why being Mexican mattered at all, and I pushed the class to think about whether it did, and if so, why:

CARTER: I'm just, like, what does it matter, like, so much—if they actually classify themselves as being Mexican, why does it matter?

DR. B.: So what do you think? Why does it matter?

CARTER: I don't know.

DR. B.: To you, you're saying it doesn't matter, right?

CARTER: Right, it doesn't matter, like, if you're, like, Mexican enough, like, or you're American enough, or if you're Canadian enough. It doesn't—it doesn't matter, . . .

DR. B.: Carter's questions are rhetorical, so she's like, "It doesn't matter if you're Mexican enough," . . . but for some reason it matters to them, so what is it about it that matters to them?

It's a question that was raised in both classes that read the book, and one that was responded to, in both classes, by drawing on personal albeit tangential experiences.

Rhys, who identified as white, reflected on their experiences living in New Mexico in a predominantly Latino community. They said, referencing their journal,

RHYS: In the younger generation of Mexicans, there's a thing that goes around where they'll be like, "Oh you're not Mexican," and generally if you don't speak Spanish . . . and you're light skinned, you're not—

DR. B.: You don't count as real Mexican.

RHYS: Yeah, you're not. People will actually, like, bully you when you're younger if you're not Mexican enough and it is a huge race battle, kind of, between what kind of Hispanic or Latino, or whatever you want to call it, you are.

Thus, Rhys explained that in some communities being Mexican enough came with real, embodied consequences for young people. It could make the difference between being bullied or not.

Yanika drew on her brother's experience to respond to Carter's rhetorical and my literal question directly. She said,

I don't know, like, why it matters to [Ari and Dante], but I have, like, kind of [inaudible] it. So my brother, he bought a truck, and he packed up his truck to move it to Arizona, . . . and the area where he's buying his house there are a lot of, like, Mexicans, or like Spanish-speaking people, so like, when he bought this truck, he was like, um, "It's kind of Mexican," like,

"I'm going to fit in with this truck," and I was like, I don't really know what he's saying. [*laughs*] Like, what does that mean? But it's like a big, red truck, and it was also a Ford, like, yeah, so [inaudible]. Because he thought that would make him fit in or something.

In this way, Yanika explained that being Mexican enough came with embodied consequences for her adult brother, too, even though he was not Mexican. These consequences were not about being bullied, but they were about fitting in to a community to which he was new.

Across these conversations, students both pulled themselves toward and pushed themselves away from Mexican American people. Darby pulled herself toward Mexican Americans by engaging in the story of nuance and complexity regarding Mexican American identities, which she said is "really cool." Rhys and Yanika pulled themselves toward Mexican Americans by drawing on their and their families' experiences in close geographic proximity to such communities. Yanika pulled herself toward Mexican Americans, first, by being careful and checking her potential racism and, second, by recognizing the importance of names, language, and sexuality in terms of existing within a racialized community. Kimberly recognized the importance of education in Mexican American communities. Stephanie and Carter, however, pushed themselves away. Stephanie did this by failing to understand the joke between the boys out of fear of being racist. Carter did this by wondering why the characters' Mexican American identities even matter. What I am not saying is that Stephanie and Carter were racist against Mexican Americans and the others were not. Instead, I am saying, in these moments in time, Darby, Yanika, Rhys, and Kimberly pulled themselves closer to understanding and embracing diverse Mexican American communities, whereas Stephanie and Carter did not. In moving closer, those students opened up opportunities for future antiracist encounters.

Differences, Tensions, and Power Dynamics within Students' Own Racialized Communities

Examining the nuances of the racialized communities represented in *Aristotle and Dante Discover the Secrets of the Universe* (Sáenz, 2012) provoked the classes to discuss such complexities in their own communities. Just as Dante doesn't feel Mexican enough, Carter didn't feel Black enough, as she shared in the following exchange:

> CARTER: Actually, now that I think about it, I get that. Especially because like, like there's a high stereotype of what kind of, like, music Black people are supposed to listen to. I'm like, I don't think this—I meet this requirement at all, like, I don't like—I'm not into, like, this scene, like entertainment-wise. I don't like the same styles of dress or anything like that, like. I just don't meet them at all, and so like, yeah, that does like center me away, like especially when I went to a predominately Black school, I was like, "I can feel the hate radiating off of all these people toward me" because of—simply because of, like, I just don't—I don't really . . . I didn't meet this stereotype [of] Black people that all of, like, like the majority of the school met, and, like, I don't know. It did cause a lot of problems for me when I went to school.

> DR. B.: So how being Black was constructed in particular context didn't align with the way you expressed being Black.

> CARTER: Yeah!

Carter's account resonated with Vic.

> VIC: I, like, relate to that a lot because in middle school I also went to a predominately Black school, and, um, it was—it makes—it makes you feel a little bit uncomfortable. I was very uncomfortable because I did not, like, I didn't speak the same, I didn't know what slang terms, I didn't curse, like, at all. I was such a good kid, and, like, it was ridiculous. I just wasn't very, like—I don't know. I didn't really like rap music, all like that.

> DR. B.: So you kind of weren't kind of meeting the expectations?

> VIC: I was not meeting expectations.

> DR. B.: And how did it feel?

VIC: It just—hey, you can definitely feel left out; you definitely, um, it's harder to make friends, and, like—I just got this, like, all the time, whenever I would just hear, "Are you even Black?," like, "You're such a white person." And stuff like that.

Both Carter and Vic identified as Black, but both of them had experienced, in school, feeling not Black enough in predominantly Black contexts, to the point of having their racial identities doubted and even being hated. Both seemed to experience both a push and a pull in relation to Black people and communities. They were rejected by some Black people but seemed to want to find and be in Black communities, just not with those who rejected them.

Yanika, as a biracial young woman, reported getting "both sides of it." She said,

It's weird, like, I get both sides of it, . . . people don't really, like, hate me if I don't, like, do something. They're like, "Oh, okay," so like, if I don't know a slang term some people will be like, "Oh, well, that's because you're white." . . . They, like, rationalize it like, "Well, oh, well you're mixed, so you don't know that, but I'll teach you and now you'll know!" And, like, they're like, "Oh, did you hear that new Taylor Swift song?" I'm like, "No." And they're like, "Well, that's because you're half-Black. But, you know, I'll play it for you and now you'll know."

Whereas Carter and Vic conveyed feeling excluded as a result of not being Black enough as Black people, Yanika conveyed feeling patronized for not being Black or white enough as a biracial person. That she felt patronized rather than tutored per se was evident when I followed up about how she felt. She said, "It doesn't, like, hurt my feelings or anything because, I mean, they're not lying, I am, like, biracial, but I don't think that, like, I don't know something because I'm mixed. . . . That's not why I haven't heard the song yet. Like I haven't been home [to hear the song]." Like Carter and Vic, Yanika experienced both a pull and a push. The pull was in being taught what it took to be Black or white, but the push was in how this felt demeaning to her as a biracial person.

Yanika reflected on what she heard among the people of color in her class:

YANIKA: Isn't it weird when we have, like, so many examples of this stuff? . . . It's actually kind of sad, like—

CARTER: Right, right. It's just, like, life though. . . .

YANIKA: I'm just trying to live my life.

CARTER: Free!

YANIKA: That's all I wanted to do.

CARTER: Right! I did not sign up for this.

Here, Yanika and Carter acknowledged the desire to live their lives free of the constraints of racialized communities, not the communities themselves, and the disappointment in being unable to do so. Thus, they were not pushing themselves away from those communities as much as understanding the ways that they did not belong among them and, perhaps, underneath, trying to figure out ways they could. In doing so, they were not closing down a future in those communities, but nor were they opening one up. Instead, they were just wondering whether there were any possibilities.

People sometimes felt pushed out of racialized communities that they expected to be a part of, and this feeling was propelled by the internalization of the fallacy of white supremacy, that is, when a person of color has received so many negative messages about their own racialized community or communities that they start to believe and make use of those messages. In Kendi's (2019) words, "Racist ideas make people of color think less of themselves, which makes them more vulnerable to racist ideas" (p. 6). Desiree alluded to the internalization of the fallacy of white supremacy when she said, "You're either light-skinned and perfect or you're nothing at all. Like the darker you are, the less you matter. . . . Because our community, like, since slavery, it was if you're lighter, you're a house slave, and if you were darker, you were out picking cotton. So, we've been taught that our whole lives." Desiree, however, was actively rejecting such an understanding of herself.

Khalil, though, seemed to struggle with it, particularly, as a Black, gay young man. I read Khalil as African American, but when I explicitly asked him about his racial identity, he said, "I'm Puerto Rican. I'm white. I'm Black. I'm Jamaican and Irish." He explained that people often interpreted this to mean he's African American, but he would respond, "Nope. Mixed, other." In a later interview, he said that his mother was Puerto Rican and Black and his biological father, who was not who he called his dad, was white and Black. He reported that his biological father asked him why he didn't "consider [him]self Black," and Khalil replied saying, "First off, that's what other people do, and I don't like it because I know I'm more than that, and I don't want to just be seen as, 'well, because your dark skin, you're Black.' No. There's more to me." He explained that claiming this complex racial, ethnic, and national identity allowed him to understand his race beyond skin color. He said claiming a Black identity resulted in being stereotyped: "I think, like, that's the hardest part about, the part of being Black, I think, because everybody put a stereotype. 'Oh your dad's not here, you guys are going to be on welfare and Section 8.'" Alternatively, by claiming a Puerto Rican identity, he could reject stereotypes of being "more privileged," as one might when understood as white, or having "live[d] in the projects." Instead, he said, "I feel going Puerto Rican, I'm just straight in the middle." In doing so, he shifted from a racial identity to a racialized national identity.

However, in conversation about the first 2016 panel discussion focused on race, which centered around Black identities, Khalil seemed to move toward claiming a Black identity. Initially, Khalil stated, "I'm not even fully Black, but it upset me." Thus, he described himself as only partially Black, but then he used first-person plural pronouns to indicate he included himself among Black people, noting that those who reacted to the panel were "criticizing us." He went on to say that "we're known as thugs." Then he said, "People make fun of Black people because of how big their lips are," and Jenna corrected him, saying, "Yeah, how big our lips are." Khalil picked up on the correction and continued, "How big our butts" are. Thus, Khalil, with a push from Jenna, pulled himself toward Black communities across these conversations about being Black in a racist society.

But Khalil was not only raced; he was, in his words, "more than that." When I asked him whether he identified as gay, he said, "Mhm. Very." The first time we discussed being both Black and gay was in class early in the semester. He said, about Black people, "It's a different race, period. No, but along with race, homophobia—like, Black people hate—they just hate gay people. So, it's just, like, they see another Black gay guy and they just automatically harass them. And then, you know, if you see a white gay guy, and they're all straight and white, they might just ignore him. And they might say something slick, but it's not as bad. And Hispanics, I don't really know." This led to Delilah talking about homophobia among "Hispanics," which she tied to Catholicism. I then asked whether the homophobia Khalil experienced might also be tied to religion, and he said, "No, not really. Like, sometimes, but most of the time, no. It's just douchebags. Like, what was it? One time I was walking and I was just—I had, like, shorts and sneakers on . . . and they were just making comments, and, like, . . . it's just like, for what? I don't even know you, but you see what you want, so just go ahead and start talking smack. . . . They still don't know nobody, but they're still talking smart." Trying to disrupt what I had come to understand as a damaging stereotype, I asked the class, "Does anybody have a different experience around? Or is that consistent with other peoples' experiences?" But Khalil responded immediately:

KHALIL: One thing they do, though—

DR. B.: Who's "they"?

KHALIL: Like, Black people. They are so okay with lesbians. Their best friend could be a lesbian, but, like, if a gay guy walked by—

Here, he stated that lesbians were absolved from what he experienced as the homophobia of Black communities, and when he referred to people in Black communities, he used third person, "they" and "their," effectively pushing himself away from Black communities and, importantly, the homophobia he understood to be within. Later, in our concluding interview, I asked him more about his description of homophobia in Black communities: "So, I just remember y'all talking about homophobia looks different in different racial and ethnic communities, and I think I heard, I might be wrong, but I thought I heard [Khalil] say, I think I heard you say that African American communities were more homophobic. But I might be wrong on saying that. And I, I guess I wanted a chance to unpack that. Like I want to talk about that." Khalil replied by first talking about the homophobia he had experienced in his family and then more publicly. He said,

Okay, so. Um, my dad's side of the family are more like, African American Black than my mom's. So, like, I went out there this summer, and they finally got to seeing me after eight years . . . and my auntie, who I used to be very close to . . . I finally got to see her and I went to go hug her, and she just walked right past me. . . . And I was just like, okay, maybe she didn't recognize me? Because when she'd seen me I was small. And then my uncle Tito, he recognized me, he was talking to me. But I was like, okay. But if I'd go on the street, and a random Black guy sees me, and he's just like, "You're a fag." And, um, everything else. So, in the book that is not okay; I'm just like, "Thanks, tell me something I don't know about myself." . . . So I think, like, if I walk past a Caucasian person, they're going to look at me and keep going. It's not a problem. But like the whole African American Black, or the Latino-Hispanic, that also is like a big one . . . it's like, the Latino race, they're just like, "I don't understand it." . . . So they'll probably get, think of stereotypes, have negative comments, but it's not like when a Black person does it. . . . It's just like, I feel like if I was to be harmed by somebody, it'll be a Black person.

When I told him that I heard "a story grounded in pain and sadness. Like your aunt not hugging you," he just said, "Yeah." Thus, I came to understand his pushing away the Black communities that included his family members as about feeling pushed out of them. His auntie refused to acknowledge him.

In a later chapter on families and parents, I share an account by Kahlil in which his pastor's wife pushed him out of the church for being too feminine. He pushed away from part of his family and from his church to protect himself from acts like being denied by his auntie and pastor's wife. To make such a difficult push, he bought into some ideas based on the fallacy of white supremacy, like Black people being on welfare, in public housing, and more homophobic than other racialized people, particularly white people. Further, Khalil bought into the idea that if he were going to be harmed, it would be by a Black person. I am reminded of how fearing Black bodies is racist, regardless of the body that experiences that fear. This, Kendi (2019) argues, is "the real Black on Black crime" (p. 8). So Khalil pushed himself away from Black communities that he understood as homophobic based on a history of having been pushed out of Black communities that he experienced as homophobic. This meant moving farther away from family, or, in Ahmed's words, from home. Khalil's past encounters led to the ones I observed during our time together. The ones I observed were thus propelled by pain and sadness and by a drive for self-protection. This pushing away effectively closed down potential futures with Black communities that included his family and home, at least for the time being.

Moving Back and Forth between Racist and Antiracist Ideas

Some white people in the school seemed to work to remove Kendi's label of "racist," with different degrees of effort and effect. Some racially privileged people were receptive to talking across differences regarding race and racism but only if they deemed those discussions acceptable in their minds. For example, after a follow-up panel prompted by the one in which panelists discussed "white history month," I again asked how it went and was informed of the format. For this panel, there was a white man who was a teacher at the school and Shayla, a Black person who was on staff at the school. They answered questions posed anonymously by students. Darren said he loved it, that he thought it was really good. He appreciated Shayla's stories in particular; he said, "Oh my god, her stories. . . . [They were] emotional, I like started crying. I was like, 'Oh my god. I did not realize. I am so sorry.'" When I asked Delilah about this panel, she said, "I kind of thought it was great . . . it was more an actual educational, you know, meeting. . . . They were just talking. And it went smoother. Like there was no pointing fingers. . . . It was more of just like a story telling. . . . I'm pretty sure a lot people got more out of it . . . I know I did. . . . So, it was more better. I felt that ease." It seems Darren and Delilah were more receptive to discussions about race and racism when whiteness was represented, when they included stories that did not directly implicate them, and when there was a smoothness or an ease for them. In other words, they wanted to learn about race and racism but only in ways that did not provoke too much discomfort. In this way, they struggled to let go of racist ideas and thus struggled to move from racist communities. In doing so, they closed down the potential for future antiracist encounters, at least in these moments in time.

Some white people strove to embrace antiracist ideas by calling out egregious racism. This was evident when the previous year's panel focused on race, like the one discussed above, had racist fallout. The panelists for this one were the aforementioned white teacher, Shayla, a person from a nearby university, a pastor, and four students. Questions were submitted by students to their advisors, who passed them on to the facilitator, another teacher at the school. My students said the panel was mostly productive and positive, particularly the follow-up discussions in their advisories, but "there were some things after the panel that happened that were very problematic things," according to Kimberly, a white student. She named a student, a white young man, who was a senior at the school, who "made a Twitter account just to post very awful things. . . . Some very racist comments and stuff." It wasn't until the next semester, when people were still talking about this race-themed panel, that I learned that the student had "put up like a picture of a monkey and was like, 'that's a Black dude,' " according to Mac, another white student. In the moment, students did not seem to know whether he'd be held accountable, and if so, how. Darby said, "If he does not get expelled, I personally am going to be really, really upset about it because this is like the eighth time that people have gone [to administrators] about him saying inappropriate things." As it turned out, he was expelled. In this case, some white students were fervent in calling out egregious racism and expecting accountability. Thus, they moved toward antiracist communities and opened up possibilities of future antiracist encounters when the circumstances were egregious enough.

Sometimes people who were in a particular moment in time enacting antiracist ideas would try to change the ideas of those enacting racist ones. Again, consider Shayla's story. Hilary, who identified as white, said that Shayla said she was "put in handcuffs . . . because they thought she stole a car. . . . But they only thought that because she was, like, Black." This prompted the following interaction between Katherine, who identified as white, and Yanika, who identified as biracial, Black and white. From the start, Katherine asserted a racist stance, and Yanika challenged her to move from that stance:

KATHERINE: Well that was—that was kind of hard because—I meant, that's still inexcusable; you shouldn't jump the gun, but I mean if a car's plates come up as stolen. . . .

YANIKA: But it was just crazy because she was talking about, like, the feeling of when she got, like, thrown up against the car and like—

KATHERINE: Yeah, that's what—that was a bit much.

YANIKA: And like, she was like, "And I'm standing there in handcuffs." And then she started choking up, and then we all started crying.

KATHERINE: Yeah, that was sad; I know it was hard. I mean, yeah, it's hard because there's such—I think the thing that we talked about is that there's a fine line between a racist and a cop trying to do their jobs. I mean, there are times when it's clearly a cross. Officers aren't, you know, always afraid. They could be racist too; it happens.

Here Katherine reflected on the challenges for the police officer and Yanika reflected on Shayla's experience. Katherine found Shayla's story "hard" rather than comfortable, but in talking with Yanika she could see how it was "sad" and "hard" for Shayla, too, and how police officers can be racist, even though, curiously, she separated racism and fear by suggesting that some police officers are racist and others are afraid. Thus, she suggested that the ones who are afraid are just doing their jobs when they inflict violence, which is a deeply flawed—and racist—argument. Still, these students pushed each other to think about how the other—either the police officer or Shayla, as a Black person under arrest—must feel, with Yanika pulling Katherine toward a less racist perspective. One might argue that Katherine was assuming a neutral stance, but as Kendi (2019) asserts, "there is no neutrality in the racism struggle" (p. 9). This pushing, though, provoked movement, however slight.

Katherine then went into an extended story about an airline that double-booked a seat. A white person was seated first, and an African American man was asked to sit somewhere else. The man refused. She said, "He, like, got so upset, where he's like, 'They were being racist; they were trying to move me to the back of the plane like it's the back of the bus.'" I think she was trying to show how "we're in such a sensitive state," in her words, that people, like the flight attendant, can't do their jobs without being called racist. I raised the issue of how we carry histories of racism around with us:

Dr. B.: The thing about that is, I think sometimes you bring into any single interaction a whole bunch of interactions from your past— . . . And so it's not necessarily that that flight attendant was doing anything wrong, but I would want the flight attendant in that case—if there's a white person and Black person, move the white person to the back of the bus, just because there's not a history there.

Katherine: But it was a plane.

Dr. B.: I mean the plane, the back of the plane. I apologize, that was history.

Katherine: I don't know. I feel like you can do whatever. I mean, I can see why you would want to move the white just so it doesn't—

Dr. B.: It conjures this whole history of hate, you know?

Indeed, Ahmed (2012) argues, drawing on Audre Lorde, "Our bodies can remember these histories even when we don't" (p. 171). John, however, argued that histories of racism should not shape our actions in the present day, saying, "I don't see how exactly that becomes such a big thing; like, you didn't even experience it firsthand. I know there's a history and you read about it." This is not surprising, considering how, according to George Yancy, quoted by Ahmed (2012), " 'white bodies move in and out of these spaces with ease' " (p. 41), so they are less likely to understand the importance of a history of racism.

I responded by explaining it wasn't just histories of racism but current acts of racism as well. But, as a white person, I decided instead to draw on my experiences as a queer person. This is a problematic move, as Ahmed (2012) points out that "identification with sexual outsiderness is at the same time a disidentification from whiteness (a not seeing whiteness) that keeps whiteness in place" (p. 152). Still, that is what I did when I referred back to when marriage between two people of the same gender was illegal, which was less than six months prior to this conversation, and said,

It happens in my preservice teacher classes all the time—all excited about showing their ring and all, their engagement. And like—it's not that they've done anything wrong, but I'm so tired of hearing about an institution that excludes me that when they come in with that I'm just like, "Aw, come on," you know? It's not that they've said it seventeen times; it's that I've heard it 17,000 times leading up to that interaction. So not relying on somebody else's history, it's my own personal history that that person doesn't deserve to have put on them. But that—I also don't—I can't be expected to pretend that doesn't exist. That's not a realistic expectation. For me to pretend that—we call them microaggressions. So like when people do little things that, like, feel bad to you over and over and over again, they like build up and they cause people to like not get out of their seat or, you know, like whatever it is.[1]

Then, in an effort to bring the conversation back to police brutality, I said, "the tricky thing about the—around the police job is there have just been too many fatalities," and Katherine replied, "Yeah. I mean those are—to me, those are inexcusable." In this way, Katherine was fervent in her rejection of what she and I understood as egregious racism but more ambivalent in her stance toward other racist behaviors. John, who also identified as white, shared her stance, and I worked to interrogate it. Thus, Katherine and John embodied racist ideas, in this moment in time, but Katherine made some moves toward destabilizing those ideas, with Yanika's and my prodding.

Here, there was some standing firm but then some pushing and pulling from that stance. And even though there was not a great deal of movement, there was what I would call some teetering. Teetering does not open up potential future encounters like movement does, but it is more promising than a rigid stance that is neither preceded or proceeded by movement.

Sometimes, though, people espousing racist ideas talked with people espousing antiracist ideas and in doing so moved slightly from the former to the latter. One day, early in the third-semester class, we were discussing the film *Stonewall Uprising* in the History and Poetry unit. A question was raised about the difference between an uprising and a riot, which led to a discussion about the 1992 reaction to the acquittal of the police officers

---

1. *Microaggressions* is a term coined by Chester M. Pierce (1970) to describe regular acts of subtle racism, particularly against African Americans.

who beat Rodney King in Los Angeles and then the Black Lives Matter movement. Then, as if echoing an unarticulated reference to All Lives Matter, Kristy said that anyone being proud is understood as an "asshole"; moreover, if she's proud as a white person, she is understood as racist. I asked whether there was any difference between being proud as a white person and being proud as a Black person. Grace, a white young woman, spoke up louder than I ever had heard her, and ever would hear her, as it turned out. She said, "Absolutely." She explained that if she hears a white person say they're proud, she thinks, "What do you have to be proud of?" but if she hears a Black person say the same thing, she's like, "You go girl. You know what's up." Abbot, who was white, said people should be proud of their accomplishments rather than their race by implication. Delilah, who was Latina, countered him, saying being proud of your race is about being proud of your history. I said people who are oppressed are proud of surviving and fighting against oppression.

At first in the conversation, I heard less listening and learning and more commitment to firm stances. Kristy and Abbot embodied racist ideas, whereas Grace and Delilah embodied antiracist ones, but when I asked Desiree how she felt about the conversation as a whole, she felt something give. She told me,

> Yeah, I remember that conversation. Um, I was actually, that was the first time I actually had a conversation with people that weren't Black that actually was like, well how, like when Abbot was like, "Well, help me understand." That was, like, the best moment for me because you never have a conversation, like I've never had a conversation with someone that wasn't Black who understood what I went through. Or who tried to understand. They just like, "Well it doesn't matter; you should just get over" or "don't say this" and "don't say that." But when Abbot said that and the whole class was actually, like, listening, and I was just, it blew my mind because it was the first time I actually had a civilized conversation about race with people. And they tried to understand.

From Desiree's point of view, at least some non-Black students were actively trying to learn antiracist ideas by actively listening rather than dismissing or constraining her as a Black person. This was not to say that they *came* to understand, just that they *tried* to understand. And in this moment in time, Desiree valued that. In that way, these students tried to move away from racist communities toward antiracist communities with what Desiree experienced as earnestness. In doing so, they opened up the potential for future interracial antiracist encounters.

Ethical Movement with Respect to Racial Diversity in Classroom Encounters

I can certainly point to ethical movement, such as when Desiree pulled herself into the embrace of Black communities and opened up possibilities for Black joy and when Delilah drew on her experiences growing up as Mexican American to open up possibilities of educating others about the Deferred Action for Childhood Arrivals (DACA) policy. And there are more examples of ethical movement, but I can also point to unethical movement, like when Kristy, who was white, pushed Desiree, who was Black, out of a racialized conversation and effectively closed down the possibility of an antiracist encounter. There are also examples of ethical and unethical stances. An example of an ethical stance was when Desiree, Jenna, and Khalil moved toward Black communities and stood firmly there, for support and strength and with liberatory potential and intention. An example of an unethical one was when John located himself firmly among people who "judge people based on race," shutting down the possibility of antiracist encounters. To move my argument about ethical movement forward, though, I want to foreground an encounter that complicates my understanding of "ethical" as well as a collection of encounters that complicate my understanding of "movement."

The encounter that complicates my understanding of "ethical" is the one where Khalil pushed himself away from Black communities that he understood as homophobic and thus distanced himself from family and friends who he experienced as homophobic. In some ways, I understand this movement as ethical, a move of self-protection, thus empowering. In other ways, I understand it as unethical because it came at such a great cost to him, thus disempowering. I will discuss his particular situation in much more detail in chapter 5, but here I will note that this encounter made me wonder about the degree to which one can characterize movement, stances, and encounters as ethical or unethical. I continue to do so because I think there is value in the work of it, but I carry the characterizations more tenuously than I did before.

The collection of four encounters that complicate my understanding of movement are when

1. Yanika and Carter did not move toward or away from racialized communities but paused to reflect on the ways they did and did not fit in with those communities;

2. Katherine and John teetered on a racist stance as they were pushed and pulled by Yanika and others;

3. Darren and Delilah struggled to let go of racist ideas; and

4. I, as the teacher, was slow to push back on students' racism.

None of these encounters show movement, but they all show more than potential for movement; they show nascent movement, maybe. There is an agility, even if not fully actualized. There is a lack of ossification. Whether in reflection, provocation, or initiative, there is, in Ahmed's words, some give.

Chapter 4

Moving with Respect to Religion in Classroom Encounters

LGBTQ+ people and their allies often have complicated relationships with religion (Bittner, 2018). This was evident in the experiences of students who took the class and also in which students came by to borrow books but did not take the class, as I discuss in the introduction. In this chapter, I study students talking about religious institutions and reflecting on their life experiences as they read fiction and nonfiction together. The students I taught who were either religious or raised with religion were Christian, and some of those were Catholic, so they spoke most frequently, although not entirely, from these perspectives. At least one spoke about her relationship with a Muslim. But most of the talk centered around Christianity.

Ann, in talking about how some religious people try to walk the line of hating the sin of homosexuality but loving the sinner, said, "I'm going to say Christians here, because, let's be real, it's mostly Christians." In the same conversation, Carter said, "I also, um, do, like, study of religions and stuff like that, like Buddhism, Hinduism stuff. And, like, I just find it interesting because, like, in my personal opinion, it's like most of the Christian people that I know are like, 'No, this is wrong.'" In other words, in her understanding of at least Buddhism, Hinduism, and Christianity, homophobia is most pronounced among Christians.

Some students focused on Catholicism, in particular. Delilah and Kristy, for example, were raised Catholic. They spoke to same-sex romantic and sexual relationships:

DELILAH: For the most part, like, Hispanics are Catholic and Catholic—like the religion of being a Catholic, it's
[indecipherable].

KRISTY: It's, like, really big against [homosexuality].

DELILAH: It's frowned upon, and it's like you did something
completely wrong.

While most of the talk centered around Christianity, including Catholicism, not all of it did. Vic, for example, spoke about her experiences being
raised Christian and dating a girl who was being raised Muslim. She said,
"I think people, uh . . . like with Christianity and stuff, or like, if you're,
um . . . Muslim, um, I just know, like, if it's—I've only had like personal,
like, things with those two particular religions, so I don't know about other
religions, but yeah. But those ones, um . . . they're—there are going to be
negative people, um, who are like, 'That's bad,' you know, 'You're going
to go to hell,' all that stuff." Whether they were talking about Christians,
Catholics, or Muslims, students described the dynamics between LGBTQ+
people and religious communities as fraught.

According to Burack (2014), the dynamics between LGBTQ+ people and the Christian right rely on the notion of compassion, which she
conceptualizes as a " 'cultural framework' that enables the possibility of
certain kinds of discourse and action" (p. 17). She describes this action
as "between sufferer(s) and actors who are capable of responding to or
alleviating suffering" (Burack, 2014, p. 5). Although compassion might
initially seem like a healthy starting place for a relationship, it is not. For
starters, just as an actor may choose to respond to or alleviate suffering,
they may choose not to. The Christian right, in fact, regularly discerns
who is and is not deserving of compassion. With respect to LGBTQ+
people, "this means compassion toward people who resist their same-sex
desires and condemnation toward people who embrace some kind of queer
identity" (Burack, 2014, p. 8). Undergirding this discernment is a balancing
of the "divine source of compassion as well as the urgency of salvation"
(Burack, 2014, p. 14). This balancing act is not new to LGBTQ+ people
raised in Christian communities. We "grow up steeped in these traditions
and modes of feeling. As a result, we recognize the invitations to shame
and renunciation held out by antigay politics and religion" (Burack, 2014,
p. 10). Thus, we know that "calls for compassion can engender cruel con-

descension as well as harsh judgments on the moral agency of sufferers" (Burack, 2014, p. 5). We carry this knowledge with us as we move into and around religious communities.

Vic, Mac, and Ann spoke explicitly about the tension between compassion and judgment with respect to religion and LGBTQ+ people. Vic mentioned that some religious people, and again she was talking about both Christian and Muslim people, "are like, 'I love you, but you're going to go to hell. I still love you.'" This was a stance Vic, and others, did not appreciate. Mac, for example, said, "'I still love you. You're going to hell, but I still love you.' . . . Yeah. It [feels] kind of dirty, you know. Kind of like, 'You're a sinner. You're doing all these sins just for being you, but I still love you.' It's like, 'I'm going to be the bigger person and love you anyway.' I don't know—that's some shade right there." Vic and Mac, thus, pushed themselves away from religious people and communities who judge them for their sexual and gender identities, even when that judgment is framed in love.

Ann, though, was not only near those people and communities, she was among them. She said,

> I used to, I don't want to say preach, because I was never a preacher, but I . . . I used to totally be behind the whole "love the sinner, hate the sin" approach before I realized that I myself was technically a sinner. I don't think I realized how—because with other sins, you know, it's not an element of identity, it's something that you do. I—you go out and steal or you go and murder, you go and commit adultery, or whatever, but it's not part of someone's identity. I don't think I realized until I started identifying as asexual and then panromantic and then homoromantic what being—a huge part it is, of yourself, of one's self. And so I think it's really hard to see; I think it's really hard for a lot . . . of Christians to see what's erroneous in that approach, because they don't understand what a huge element of people's identity it is.

It was not until she started moving herself toward queer communities that she started pulling herself out of and away from Christian communities that judged LGBTQ+ people. Such movement was not necessarily easy. Ann's history with and in Christian communities was an intimate one.

She moved away from them because she felt judged harshly as she began to claim nonheterosexual identities, but she continued to empathize with them, as evident when she said, "I think it's really hard for a lot . . . of Christians." In other words, the break was not a clean one. It was complicated by deep struggles between religious and sexual identities. It was a move away from a sort of home.

Students drew on their experiences with religion and religious people and connected to the literature we read in class to move both farther away from religious people and institutions, when they experienced religion as punishment, and closer to them, when they experienced religion with a complexity that allowed for more tolerance if not acceptance. Even in these cases, the proximity often came with a cost.

Religion as Punishment

Students talked about religion in terms of punishments for behavior deemed wrong by those invested in Christian institutions, whether or not they were among them. They talked about being "hit" with Bible verses and being told they would be out of heaven or at least out of their families on religious grounds. Not surprisingly, they pushed back against such punishments, often at some expense.

In the spring of 2016, we were reading and discussing Andrews's *Some Assembly Required* and Hill's *Rethinking Normal* and preparing to write a journal entry about the books, and we were reviewing where we had left off in Andrews's book. He had just met Darien, who becomes his girlfriend, and because he has not yet come out as trans his friends and family understand the relationship as a lesbian one. His best friend, Andi, has sent him some Bible verses condemning same-sex relationships. Students were very critical of Andi and then started talking about their experiences with Bible verses. Abbot started, "I've been studying Bible verses . . . [and] my thing to do is to send them Bible verses back that basically just contradict what they say. . . . But I haven't been hit with a Bible verse in a while." At this, the class erupted in laughter, then Desiree chimed in with her experiences: "I used to get Bible verses too. . . . Because, well, I was a problem child. So my family, like most of my aunts and like, they all would like bring stuff into the—they was raised up in the church, and they were all like pastors, and any time I did something wrong, they would, like, sing [to] me about Bible verses and pray with my mom." In response, Khalil pointed at Desiree and shook his head. When I asked him about his reaction, he explained how deeply Christian his family was and then said, "So, you know, and your parents—you did something wrong and and they just want to [*slaps hand*] boom. And then they be like, 'Read this.'" I responded to his slap and "boom" with, "And that's getting hit with the Bible verse. Yeah, yeah, I hear you." Even in a different class, the one in the previous semester, while reading and discussing a different book, Kuklin's *Beyond Magenta*, Carter said, "my family was like super Christian or whatever, and they're like, 'Gay is wrong,' like, smash, smash, smash, 'You're going to hell.'" Thus, Abbot, Desiree, Khalil, and Carter talked about being if not "hit" then at least punished with Bible verses and "smash[ed]" with Christianity more broadly. Desiree and Khalil would "get" Bible verses when they "did something wrong" so that they would learn to behave as their religious family believed was right. For Carter, this was specifically tied to being gay.

Punishments, though, did not only come in being "hit" in the moment. Some came in the form of threats for the future. In a later chapter about families and parents, I write about how some family members told their queer kids they would be going to hell. Darby, for example, contrasted Ari and Dante's experience coming out to their parents with her own by emphasizing their religious commitments. She said, "I grew up in like super-religious Christian churches my entire life that are like, 'Nope, gay bad. Going to hell.'" As previously mentioned in this chapter, Vic talked about Christians and Muslims telling gay people they are going to hell, and Carter talked about her Christian family saying something similar. Also, when I asked the class about their experiences with the "relationship between empathy and religion" in our discussion of Cameron in Kuklin's *Beyond Magenta*, Mac said decidedly that religious people were not empathetic people. They explained, "My grandparents are, like, that religious. They're like, 'You're not allowed to be gay because you're going to hell.' That's the thing that they are. . . . Yeah. That's the kind they are." It was certainly a prominent even if not surprising theme across class discussions that many students talked about knowing at least Christians, if not religious people more broadly, who believed and espoused that LGBTQ+ people were going to hell.

Sometimes, though, students talked about LGBTQ+ people being ousted from home instead of heaven. We were reading and discussing

Farizan's *If You Could Be Mine* in the fall of 2015, and I asked students to select characters they identified with and explain why. Vic selected both the main character, Sahar, and her love interest, Nasrin:

> VIC: I think that I really, I can connect with Sahar and Nasrin. . . . Because, okay, because like . . . I dated someone who came from like a Muslim type of family. . . . So it was like—it was very hard, so it was like, [she] didn't see us dating any time, like, past high school. So like that was, like, hard for me because, like, I was saying, "Oh my God, I'm so in love." And then, you know. But like, we're still friends so [indecipherable].

> DR. BLACKBURN: Okay, so [her family] knew you were dating?

> VIC: . . . No, they would have killed her . . . because it's just, like, not even a thing, like—it, I don't know. She was saying, like, in her religion, like nobody is open about that. . . . Unless, like, you just don't want to see your family ever again. But like, oh. . . . But also Nasrin because I feel like—I, um—it's like, I don't know, it's like we can date, but then it's like eventually you feel like you're going to have to just do what your parents want you to do, which is sad.

In this account, Vic described her relationship with her middle school girlfriend, who was Muslim, saying if her family knew she was dating a girl they would excommunicate her from the family forever. Whether young people were getting ousted from heaven or home, they were being pushed away both by and from religion, religious institutions, and religious people.

In these encounters, students described being judged harshly by religious people and communities because of their sexual and gender identities, or even because of their acceptance of others' sexual and gender identities. As a result, they pushed themselves away from these communities, even when those communities played a significant role in their growing up. As they pushed themselves away from these communities, they moved themselves toward LGBTQ+ communities, whether as allies or as LGBTQ+ people. Such movement suggests that they experienced their religious communities and LGBTQ+ communities as mutually exclusive, closing down the possibility of embracing both religious and queer identities.

The Push, the Pull, and the Sacrifice

Students often pushed back against or pushed away from what they understood to be religiously based homophobia and transphobia. Abbot drew on the Bible to do so. He said, "I know [the Bible] well enough to know that for every statement that seems like it discriminates someone, there's another statement that totally throws it out and just makes it not worth it." He went on to talk about how that plays out in terms of discrimination against gay people. He said, "People use religion as, like, an excuse for, like, homophobia all the time. But even though there is, like, one line in the Bible that it says something to that nature—like, I know it's an interpretation. But it also says, before anything else, treat your fellow man kindly. So, like, using your religion as an excuse for homophobia, or any sort of hatred or shade, if you will, is just kind of, like—I don't understand it because, before anything, you're just supposed to treat people kindly." Delilah immediately affirmed Abbot, saying, "You're supposed to love thy neighbor," and Abbot continued, "Even if they did say it a million times in the Bible and just stressed, like, that homosexuality . . . is forbidden—even if people did take that as, like, if you are homosexual, they'd take that as, like, being—like, violating religion or being disrespectful of religion—still, it still said in the Bible that you combat disrespect . . . you combat violence and hate, still, with, like, peace and love." Here Abbot and Delilah, both of whom were raised Catholic, both of whom are straight and cisgender, critiqued people who used the Bible to condemn homosexuality rather than to promote kindness, peace, and love. Thus, they pushed away from a particular embodiment of Christianity while pulling themselves toward an alternative. In doing so, they opened up the possibility of a Christian future, but one that is distinct from the Christian past they had experienced.

Whereas some people struggled with such tensions, pushing away judgment and pulling toward love, some left their religious homes entirely. John, for example, said, "The only time I've ever actually encountered someone that's, you know, not really, uh, pro-LGBT is my current priest at my, what I used to call my church." John did not mean that he had never encountered homophobes and transphobes; he meant he had not in his religious communities, but when he did, recently, in his church's leadership, he stopped calling the church *his* church. Thus, he pushed himself away from the religious institution he had formerly claimed as his own.

Students also recognized, though, that religious people are diverse, that they are, according to Mac, not all like that. Mac said, "But not all people who are religious are like that, I've learned. But, you know, and it's very easy to be like, 'Everyone who's religious is homophobic, but that's not true.'" Carter underscored this point, particularly in reference to Catholics. She said, "My best friend's family is Roman Catholic, but they're cool with the LGBT community. . . . When it doesn't say anything against it, they're like, 'Hey, I'm cool with everything.'" Clearly Carter experiences her best friend's family as queer-friendly. What is less clear is what the first "it" references—maybe the Bible, maybe the Catholic Church, although both of these are interpreted at least by some people as prohibiting homosexuality. Still, this was not the interpretation of Carter's best friend's family, at least as Carter experienced them. This allowed Carter, as someone who identified as pansexual, to be close to this friend and their family. It allowed her to move closer to Catholicism.

Carter valued an openness when it came to religion, even beyond the issues it raises for LGBTQ+ people. This was evident when we were reading and discussing *Aristotle and Dante Discover the Secrets of the Universe*. We were toward the beginning of the novel, and to help students connect with the characters I asked them to "write about a time something really challenged you or something with which you deeply struggled." In response, Carter wrote and shared with the class her having become more open-minded about religion in general and her desire for her family to share in that openness. She explained, "My parents were always like, 'Well, our religion is right; every other religion is wrong,' like plain and simple, but, like, without an—like without directly saying that and, like, just based on how they thought about different things and stuff like that. It was very evident, and just, like, I always felt like that was wrong. Like, it—it—like, because I'm in the mindset, it's like, 'Who are you to say that to somebody that what they believe in is wrong because you don't believe in it?'" She said her doubts in her parents' sense of righteousness was amplified when she took a human geography course in the previous school year. She said it "was really interesting because, like, we learned about, like, different aspects of other people's cultures and their religions and stuff like that, and I like the study of, like, human geography in general, and it's like a real, like, way more open on, like, just what people believe in." Understanding religion in this way drew Carter to it. It seemed to feel right to her in a way that her parents' embodiment of religion did not. She not only liked it, she claimed it as her own when she said she wrote this journal entry about her "religion open-mindedness." It pulled her closer to religion and religious people.

And yet, often the push and the pull were in tension with—not isolation from—each other. Consider Ann's account, for example. We, as a class, were talking about a meme a student brought in that pictured two figures like you sometimes see on public restroom doors to indicate who is expected use that particular room. But the figures were not white or black, which is typical. Instead, one was in what looked like a Confederate flag, and the other was in what looked like a rainbow flag. The Confederate one was kicking the rear end of the rainbow one. There was some discussion of whether the Confederate flag represented homophobia and transphobia, among other oppressions, particularly racism. John asserted it did not. He said it represented rebellion. Others said they understood the flag to be a declaration of white supremacy and racism but also other oppressive values, including homophobia and transphobia. I wondered aloud how John might feel when some people understood that flag to represent values that he did not hold, and Ann replied, "I feel that a lot because I've been raised in a Christian home . . . [and] there are other people going around like being all Christian, shouting all these terrible things, and I'm sitting here like [indecipherable]." I understood Ann to mean that she felt uncomfortable, at least, claiming a Christian identity when some Christians espoused hateful values that conflicted with her own. She worried about being thought to be a hateful Christian.

Some students who identified as both Christian and LGBTQ+ struggled with the tensions between the two. You might recall from the first chapter when Sherry talked about being raised in a Christian home and attending Christian camps when she started experiencing "same"-sex desire. She told about being taught it was a sin and feeling horrible, she talked about crying and praying to be straight, but she also talked about making out with another lesbian camper during this same period of time. The irony was not lost on her. Vic articulated a similar struggle:

Vic: I think it's really hard for, um, me personally to, especially when I first came out, like, after—sort of kind of during eighth grade, yes—

Dr. B.: And at that point you came out as—

VIC: Oh, bisexual. . . . It was really hard, because then I started questioning my religion as well, because I was like, "Well, people keep telling me I'm going to go to hell, so I don't think I should be a Christian anymore." . . .

DR. B.: So are you at a peaceful place in your questioning that?

VIC: No, no.

DR. B.: So you're kind of still in the midst of it all.

VIC: Yeah, like I still, like if someone were to ask me if I was a Christian, I'd be like, "Sure." But it's like, I don't know really, because it's like it's hard for me to say I'm a Christian and I tell them I'm gay. And then they're like, "What? No." And then it's like—

DR. B.: Like the two are conflicting.

VIC: Right, 'cause it's like, Why can't I be a Christian and gay?

Here, Vic wondered whether she could be both Christian and gay but also wondered why she could not be. She was, at the time, still in a place of questioning the relationship between the two. There was both a push away from Christianity and a pull toward it. And this tension was hard on Vic. She said, "It's just a lot. It makes it really hard for people, I feel; it makes it really hard for people because it's like, well now I need to rethink everything I do." Although she talked first about it being hard for "people," as if it could be anyone, she shifted to first-person singular pronouns after that; she suggested it's hard for her because it demands that she "rethink everything." I agreed in parallel. That is to say, I first said how it could be for people and then in second-person singular, in reference to her. I said, "Right, it can be really tumultuous for people. Yeah, it's like you're giving up a lot." Thus, students pushed themselves away from religious communities and pulled themselves toward LGBTQ+ communities, but they recognized that this movement came at a cost, and they actively questioned why they could not be in both communities. In this questioning, they imagined the possibility of being able to be in both religious and queer communities.

Khalil

These tensions were ones Khalil talked about at length. Khalil, whom I've discussed in previous chapters, is the student I read as Black but who explained to me explicitly that he was multiracial. That said, he regularly implicitly identified with Black people. The tension with religion, however, was around his sexual identity and gender expression. With respect to sexuality, Khalil had recently shifted from identifying as bisexual to identifying as gay, and he talked about having boyfriends. In terms of gender, he preferred masculine pronouns. He performed femininity sometimes but not always. In our introductory interview, he said,

> I wear makeup, I put extensions in, I wear skinny jeans, I like clothing that fits me. First off, I've been wearing tight clothes since I was in my emo stage, so tight clothing has just always been there. But now I'm starting to get into colorful stuff, and this year I was like, I need my hair to grow faster; I'm tired of putting heat in it; I'm going to put extensions in. . . . And it's hard because, like, some days—like, the other day I was wearing baggy jeans and T-shirt and a hoodie and sneakers.

Sometimes he performed masculinity for safety's sake—to ride public transportation, for example—but other times just because he wanted to. I heard him identify as male, as a feminine male, and as not female. When he recounted wearing a dress and heels, he described himself as being in drag. So, he performed gender variably, but, as he said, "it's hard." This difficulty extended to his relationship with religion.

In our final interview, Khalil described himself as a "total Christian" and a "little church boy." In class, he talked about how church used to be for him: "Sunday, Tuesday, Wednesday, and Thursday, and you got to go back on Saturday to go back on Sunday, and then you got night church." But, he told me, "I just don't go to church no more." He explained that he prayed every day and listened to gospel music all the time because, in his words, "it kind of relieves me."

Khalil talked about how important this community had been to him. He "loved" both the pastor and his wife. Because of them, he thought, "Okay, I can deal with these type of people." He said when he was feeling suicidal he choreographed a dance to Beyoncé's "I Was Here." He described the song as about death and explained that he "connected it all to my thoughts of suicide." He decided to share the performance with his pastor because, in Khalil's words, "I connected to him so much. He taught me how to play the drums; we have the same birthday. He was just like a grandfather to me." The pastor responded positively, saying "I like it" and "I'm glad you're still here, and if anytime you need to talk, we can talk." Further, Khalil "loved" the pastor's wife, and showed her the same dance. Rather than responding with empathy, she told him, "'You need to listen to more masculine music, more gospel music, uh, you have all these spirits around you, I need them to go. . . . If you're going to still contribute to this lifestyle, you can't be here.'" According to Khalil, the pastor's wife was "trying to take the demons out of me," and the pastor was talking with Khalil's dad. Khalil thought, "Okay. I can't do this." In our initial interview, he told me, "That was the actual first church that I really got into that I loved so much, and I got kicked out." In this case, Khalil left the church rather than changing his sexual identity and gender expression. He pushed the religious institution, or the homophobic weaponization of Christianity, away.

That said, he described going back to church, albeit a different one. He was out of the state for the summer, visiting family, and he was expected to go to church for his nephew's christening. He decided, "I'm going to be there to support him." But then he started asking about and encouraging his sister-in-law to go to church with him. He said, "I was like, 'We're going to church, so get dressed.' And I have no problem going to church, and I went there, and it was just like nobody knew [I was gay], and it's like everything was just gone, and I was able just to focus on what I came to do. And I'm like, 'I wish it was like that all the time.'" In this case, Khalil preferred to conceal his sexual identity rather than sacrifice his faith. He pulled closer to religion at this moment in time, and, in an effort to do so, he suppressed at least his sexual identity and likely his gender expression, although he did not mention that specifically. Across his accounts, I see the push, the pull, and the sacrifice of his sexual identity, his gender expression, and his religious commitments. He pushed away from a Christianity of judgment and pulled himself toward LGBTQ+ communities, but then he also pulled himself toward a Christianity of home, and, to avoid its judgment, he pushed himself away from LGBTQ+ communities, at least in moments in time. He longed for a future in which he could be in both communities simultaneously, even though his present did not allow for it.

Ethical Movement with
Respect to Religion in Classroom Encounters

The students in the LGBTQ+-themed literature classes talked most of Christianity among the religions, sometimes with particular attention to Catholicism. Sometimes they spoke of Islam, not only with respect to Vic's ex-girlfriend but also in relation to Farizan's *If You Could Be Mine*. Regardless, students reported being pushed away from religion, religious institutions, and religious people. They did not report being pulled toward such institutions and people except where they were not understood as LGBTQ+. Moreover, students reported pushing themselves away from religion, religious institutions, and religious people when they understood the related values as hateful ones, such as homophobic and transphobic ideas. Much less frequently, when they understood religious values as loving and accepting ones, students reported pulling themselves closer to the people and institutions who held them. For those whose religious commitments were deeply ingrained, such a push-and-pull relationship was trying if not damaging. Undergirding them seemed to be a longing for a future in which they could exist in both religious and queer communities.

I understand all of the movement initiated by young people, whether moving toward or away from religious or queer communities, as ethical because they were agile in looking for love and home and wanting to find both in both communities. It is in the push and the pull of religious institutions that I saw unethical encounters, whether the religious institution was pushing away LGBTQ+ people or pulling only particular, "deserving," to use Burack's (2014) language, people toward them. These unethical encounters closed down the possibility of future encounters where people could exist in both religious and queer communities simultaneously, whereas the ethical encounters initiated by the young people opened up the possibility of such futures. Further, encounters where a person could benefit from being in LGBTQ+ and religious communities simultaneously would be much more ethical than those that demand a person be pushed and pulled between them, giving up something of themself in each movement. Something similar can be said of families, which I explore in the next chapter.

Chapter 5

Moving with Respect to Families in Classroom Encounters

I was struck most by students' shifting relationships with families, and with parents in particular. When I talk about families and parents, I am using the words as they were used by my students and the literature we read and discussed together. I am not particularly interested in who was born to or adopted by whom, unless my students were. I am only interested in whom my students understood as parents and family in the literature and their lives. With this notion of parents and family, I look at how students moved farther away from them by critiquing them through literature we read and discussed together as well as through their stories about their lives beyond the classroom. I also look at how they moved closer to parents and families by striving to understand parents' grief and fear in relation to their children's sexual and gender identities and appreciated them for loving, affirming, and standing up for them.

Critiquing Parents

Students critiqued parents and families in the literature we read and discussed together, such as *Fun Home, Rethinking Normal,* and *Some Assembly Required.* They also critiqued parents and families they encountered in their jobs, their friends' homes, and their own homes.

In Course Literature

In the third of the three semesters, we read several excerpts from the graphic memoir *Fun Home: A Family Tragicomic* (Bechdel, 2006) and listened to the related songs from the eponymous musical (Kron & Tesori, 2015) as well as part of an interview with Alison Bechdel, Lisa Kron, and Jeanine Tesori conducted by NPR's Terry Gross (2015). (For more about this lesson, read Blackburn, 2019.) *Fun Home* is a graphic memoir of Bechdel's growing up and coming out in a funeral home with her family that pays particular attention to Bechdel's father, who experienced and embodied same-sex desire throughout his life and ultimately died by what might have been interpreted as an accident but Bechdel certainly interprets as suicide. The memoir was made into a musical, which was awarded a Tony.

One of the memoir excerpts comprised two pages (pp. 220–221), each with twelve square panels (three across, four down). In each panel Alison, the college-aged daughter, and Bruce, her middle-aged father, sit together in a car. He is driving. Alison is eager to connect with her father since just coming out as lesbian, but her father is unavailable to connect with her because he is so isolated in his own internalized homophobia. The conversation is awkward and halting. The correlated song is "Telephone Wire," in which Alison struggles to talk about what it is like for both of them, daughter and father, being gay. Her father talks about his experiences as a closeted gay man, but he makes no effort to connect with her, despite her efforts. In the interview, both Bechdel and Tesori reference how painful this bit was for them to watch in the musical. Although the students did not see the musical, we discussed the related excerpt of the memoir, the song, and part of the interview, and students talked about the disconnect between daughter and father. Kristy, who identified as straight, cis, and white, said,

> The part that caught my attention the most was when [the father] was saying how when he was little he really wanted to be a girl and dressed in girls' clothes. . . . And [Alison] was like, "I wanted to be a boy, dress in boys' clothes. Remember?" And it reminded me back to the scene on this side [a scene that we had read, heard, and discussed previously where the father looks at a butch woman disdainfully], where he's like, "Is *that* what you want to look like?" And it's like he was kind

of, like, judging her for it. But, like, he did the same thing when he was little.

I heard Kristy as angry with the father for belittling his daughter for feelings he shared with her. Similarly, Desiree, who identified as straight, cis, and Black, said, "The ending of the song really stuck out because it was like 'that we're both—,' then she didn't get to say 'gay'; he, like, cut her off. So, I don't remember what he said, but he said something that had nothing to do with what she was singing about." Desiree, too, seemed angry with the father, in this case for preventing Alison for naming their both being gay. In other words, both Kristy and Desiree blamed Alison's father for putting obstacles in between his daughter and himself and therefore preventing their connection—indeed, ensuring their disconnect. So while Bruce pushed Alison away from him, Kristy and Desiree moved themselves farther from Alison's father and closer to college-aged Alison. This movement occurred across lines of difference defined by sexuality but also gender expression and, in Desiree's case, race. They moved farther away from at least one person if not people more generally who struggled with internalized homophobia and toward those who more confidently claimed their gay identities. In doing so, they closed down possibilities of connecting with people struggling with internalized homophobia while opening up possibilities of connecting with LGBTQ+ people without that struggle.

When we read and discussed *Rethinking Normal* (Hill, 2014) and *Some Assembly Required* (Andrews, 2014), students pushed away from parents by critiquing the parents represented in those books. Recall that these two autobiographies were written by trans teens who for a period of time shared a romantic and sexual relationship. *Rethinking Normal* was written by Katie Rain Hill, who transitioned to being a girl as a teenager in Oklahoma. It begins with her birth in 1994 and concludes with her attending college at the University of Tulsa. A significant thread throughout the book is Katie's relationship with Arin Andrews, the author of *Some Assembly Required*, which I describe in chapter 2.

In this class, students chose one of the two books to read, and we discussed them together. Mac, who was gender-fluid and white, had selected and read *Some Assembly Required*. They were sharing their frustration with Arin Andrews's mother's response to Arin's coming out to her as trans. According to Mac's reading of *Some Assembly Required*,

Arin's mother "was basically like, when he told her he was trans, she kind of didn't say anything; he gave her, like, a newspaper, that, you know, [indecipherable] gave about Katie Rain Hill. And he's like, you know, 'Mom, I'm not the only one. This is not just me. There are other people.' And she didn't read it. She tucked it away. She didn't read it. And she kind of just ignored it." Mac seemed appalled if not offended that Arin's mom essentially dismissed Arin's efforts to talk with her about his gender identity.

In this discussion, I asked students to focus on the parts in *Rethinking Normal* and *Some Assembly Required* where Katie and Arin were depressed and suicidal, at which points their mothers begin to take their gender identities more seriously. I asked students to find the scenes where this happens, and when a student conveyed she did not understand, I modeled with *Some Assembly Required*:

> So, in this book, what happens is, um, as, so, the, what's going on is Katie is, Katie and her family have moved to Oklahoma where her grandparents are, and she feels really isolated and depressed, and it's just a terrible move for her. And then her parents get divorced, and that, like, sends her—so she—her father had been distancing himself from her the more feminine she got. So, she missed him already, but things happened in the house just even made it like a greater loss, so she was getting more and more isolated. She did have a social group, a group of girls at her middle school who she, you know, to hang out with. . . . Okay, so she's getting really depressed, and I'm just going to read the same part we read. So—oh, and she's a big reader and writer, so she just reads and writes to escape from her reality, so she, it's great because it gives her an alternative world, but it also makes her even more isolated, right. . . . Okay, so, she tells—she finds an article online; she tells her mom, "Hey this is me, I'm trans." And her mom's like, "Oh, come on, can't you just be gay." And she's like, "No." And um, it's an Oprah interview that she gets her to, um, watch, and then these articles on trans kids.

At this point, I started to read from the book, a part where Katie's mom is talking:

DR. BLACKBURN: "'Will this make you happy, baby?'"

[*Mac hits their desk with their palm*]

DR. B.: "And I felt a rush of overwhelming relief, 'Yes,' I said, 'I think it will. I just want to be a girl.'"

[*Mac rubs their head*]

DR. B.: "'Okay,' my mom said softly and she put her arms around me. We sat there and hugged each other tight, both bawling."

[*Mac adjusts in their seat*]

DR. B.: "My mom wiped her eyes, straightened, and held onto my shoulders. 'Then we're going to do this. Make me list of everything you want done, and I will make sure I do every single thing on it.'" [*sounding choked up*] Did the same thing to me all over again. You'd think I could handle it on the third reading.

At this point, there was an audible sigh by multiple students. Carter, who identified as pan, cis, and Black, said, "That is so sweet." I continued reading:

DR. B.: "'Really?' I said. 'You just have to promise me one thing.'"

[*Mac puts their hand over their heart*]

DR. B.: "'What?' I said, wiping my nose. 'You cannot kill yourself.'"

[*Mac slams their palm on the desk*]

DR. B.: "'I can't help you, I can't fix this if you kill yourself. You've got to promise me that no matter how hard it gets, you will not take your life.'"

[*Mac makes a sort of namaste pose*]

DR. B.: "I looked at my mom, her green eyes wet and bloodshot from crying. 'I promise.' I said."

[*Mac rubs their face, puts their head down, and shakes their head*]

DR. B.: " 'Okay. You hold your promise. I swear I'll hold mine.' "

Carter said, "Aw, that was so cute. I know, right? That was the cutest, oh my god." Here, I contextualized and read the scene where Katie's mother begins to support her in her transition. In doing so, I conveyed emotion, getting a bit choked up as I read. I think it is fair to say I was connecting with and moving toward the mother, as a mother myself. But Carter also described the scene as "sweet" and "cute," and other students felt similarly, as indicated by their collective sigh. I understood Mac's gestures as engagement and appreciation; I understood them as being moved by Katie's story and toward Katie's mother.

At least the three of us, and likely others in the class, moved across lines of difference toward Katie's mother. Mac crossed lines of difference defined by gender identity, and Carter crossed lines of difference defined by race. But most pertinent here is that both of them crossed lines of difference defined by their roles in families, that is, as children moving toward Katie's mother. In doing so, they opened up the possibility of moving closer to parents of trans kids; in the case of Mac, this included their own.

Then, Vic volunteered to share the parallel scene from *Some Assembly Required*. She explained first that Arin had been cutting himself with a knife and considering suicide. She said, reading,

"The next night was more of the same, and on the third day I was lying on the bed staring at the ceiling and mom came in and sat down next, beside me. She saw the knife still on the floor, and picked it up. 'This trans stuff is real, isn't it?' She asked. 'It's not going away, you're not going to grow out of it.' 'No, I'm not.' 'But how are you going to live like this?' 'Would you ignore the fact that this is who I am makes me think that life isn't worth living at all?' She looked at me and then glanced back down at the knife. 'You really would have done this?' She asked. 'I tried.' She nodded and tears started streaming down her cheeks, down her neck. 'I will support you. I won't lose you.' 'You won't.' I said, 'I'm still me, I'll always still be me. But I need my body to be my own.' She nodded again. And I knew that she finally got it."

Throughout Vic's reading, Mac was still, with face resting on fist and elbow resting on desk. They appeared to be listening, but they were still. They were the first to raise their hand to speak afterward. Their contribution was stumbling, a bit hard to follow. I could hear their frustration with Arin's mother when they said she "doesn't accept him for who he is. . . . If she can't accept him for who he is. . . . He might have actually gone through with it. She would have lost a son." Yanika, who identified as straight, cis, and biracial, agreed, saying, "I feel like if the knife wasn't there in the situation at all, then she wouldn't, if—like she wouldn't have come to that—not, like, realization. . . . I feel like that if the knife wasn't there and Arin didn't feel at that point, then [his suicide] would have happened." Here, Mac and Yanika suggested that if the mother had not seen the knife, then Arin might very well have died from suicide. I, likely identifying with the mother, said, "But it's a game changer, right?" But Katherine, who identified as bi, cis, and white, rejected my excusing the mother. She said, "I feel like it should not have gotten to that point; I'm like, as a parent you really should realize that your child is going to commit suicide. . . . I just don't understand why it has to be so extreme." This time I understood. I said, "Right, why can't you just listen to me before I get to that point," and Katherine continued, "Right, it's almost like, you don't believe them, you don't believe your own child saying these things to you; it's kind of hard to deal with, you know, not getting the audience you need from your parents." And, again, I understood, "Right. Right. I think that's a good point." Interestingly, both Katherine and I started talking to Arin's mother using second person, "you." I then started using first person, as if I were Arin. In doing so, I shifted closer to Arin and farther from his mother. Katherine first referred to Arin in third person, using "them," but then second person, "you," when she said "not getting the audience you need from your parents"; this also suggests a shift closer to Arin. Mac mentioned something they saw on social media "that was about trans equality, and it was like, when you're pregnant, you don't know what gender your child's going to be. And, but you still love them, so why should it matter now? [indecipherable]. It wasn't exactly like that, but that was the gist of it." By referring to the parents of trans youth in second person here, Mac moved closer to Arin's mother while moving no farther away from Arin. Thus, Mac, Yanika, and Katherine pushed themselves away from Arin's mother, and I let go, a bit, of my tightly held grip on the mothers. But then Mac made a sort of turn back toward mothers of trans youth, a movement, even if just for a moment. Here we see an ambivalence, a desire to connect with parents of trans youth but an unwillingness to tolerate transphobia from them, a possibility of connecting but not without some constraints that protect trans youth.

AS TEACHERS BEYOND CLASS

Students also critiqued the parents they encountered beyond what we read and discussed in class, in contexts where they could position themselves as teachers. For example, one day there had been a snowstorm and students were trickling in, so we were just chatting. A student from the previous semester's class had come in and talked about her cousin's assumptions of gender in relationship to earrings, and Kristy built on that discussion. She said,

> I work at Claire's, so I, like, pierce people's ears. . . . This one lady got her son's ears pierced, and she was like, "I don't even know if I should do this, or if I do I should only get one done because I'm afraid he's going to look gay." . . . It's like that thing with the whole gender thing is either girls have their ears pierced or, and boys don't. Or boys have one—it's so stupid. . . . The world is changing, like—you have to constantly evolve and, like, adapt to new changes.

Here, Kristy critiqued a parent who worried about ear piercings making her son look gay because, as she said, "there's nothing wrong with being gay . . . it's a natural thing, like, it's something you see every day and it's—even if you didn't see it every day there's no reason to hate on it." Kristy, here, moved herself away from, and more specifically above, parents by making it clear *they* had something to learn from *her, she* had something to *teach them.*

Sometimes students talked about their friends' parents in similar ways. Mac, for example, talked about their friend's parents doing things that might be understood as minor but are also major to their friend:

MAC: They accept them and they just don't use the right pronouns. They don't accept them. They say that they do accept
them, but they don't. . . .

DR. B.: And they're, like, these little things that they do over
and over again that kind of call into question their acceptance?

MAC: Yeah.

DR. B.: Some people call those microaggressions. . . .

MAC: They'll use the wrong pronouns, use the wrong
name. . . . Their actions contradict what they say about him
and it bothers me, but they keep saying, like, the name, and,
like, I just—I try to influence them. And especially his younger
siblings. I'll be like, "That's [Francis]," or "he," you know?

DR. B.: Yeah, you model the good behavior and show them
how to do it.

Here, Mac revealed how the parents were failing their child, Mac's friend,
and Mac was not only bothered but actively tried to educate them, dis-
tinguishing themself from these parents but also attempting to educate
them. Mac tried to move them.

As Kristy and Mac positioned themselves as educators of parents,
in some ways this positioning moved them away from these parents, but
not so far away that they could not communicate across their differences.
Indeed, they stayed far enough away to distinguish themselves but close
enough together to interact, to educate. In doing so, they opened up
possibilities of ongoing communication and education.

IN THEIR FAMILIES

This dynamic was evident when students talked about parents in the
books we read as well as other parents in their lives, but it became most
pronounced when they talked about their own families. When students
critiqued their families, they effectively pushed them away from them.
Students did so by critiquing their family members' policing of gender;
their lack of knowledge regarding sexuality and gender, like perceiving it

as a phase; their dismissal of their feelings; and their loving them *despite* their sexual and gender identities.

Just as Kristy reported parents in Claire's policing their sons' gender expression through ear piercings, students reported their own family members policing gender expression as well. I had explained, early in the second-semester class, that gender policing is "where people act like, 'I need to make sure that you know how to act like a boy right' or 'act like a girl right.'" In students' accounts, as at Claire's, boys were the main focus of such policing, but it was not just parents who did it. Carter, for example, told a story about her older brothers refusing to play with her because boys don't play with girls and her younger brothers playing dolls with her but then being teased by her older brothers and corrected by her parents. She wanted playmates so would question her family members. She said,

> I'm the only girl out of—I have five brothers. So I have never had like—so I have never had a girl companion at home that I can, like, play with, like play with others. And of course like I have, like, toys and, like, Barbies and Bratz dolls, but like I can only play with them by myself. So I asked my brothers if they'd play with me—my older brothers were like, "No." But I have two younger brothers, and I could, like, talk them into playing with me, but like as, like, my brothers would like just make fun of them. Like, "What are you doing? Why are you playing with dolls?" And they're like—and like my parents would be like, "You shouldn't be doing that," but wouldn't say anything knowing that I'm the only girl, and I didn't have anyone else to play with, and I'm like, "I don't, I don't see a problem with this." So, like, all my brothers would be like, "Dude, I'm not playing with you simply because I'm not a girl, I'm a guy and I don't do that." It's like, "Well, why not?"

This prompted Yanika to tell a similar story in which her younger brothers policed her older brother for playing with her:

> YANIKA: I also have five brothers. . . . And I have two sisters. And so my older bro—my eldest brother—would be the one that played with me, and then my younger brothers would tease my older brother, saying that, like, "Oh, but you have a girlfriend and you can't do that," or something along those lines.

DR. B.: So they were the gender police?

YANIKA: Yeah. . . . So like everybody's, like, policing.

Students told stories of parents getting boys, particularly feminine boys, "in so much trouble," in Vic's words, for playing with girls, playing with dolls, and painting their nails.

Girls, too, were policed by their parents, not when they were young, but when they became older. Terry, who identified as straight, cis, and white, shared this story:

> When I was little my mom was all for, like, "everything is pretty much gender neutral." But then I got older, and then right after sophomore year, when I cut my hair, she was—like, I started doing the same things I did when I was little, but then she was like, "Why do you want to be a boy?" And I'm like, "This isn't new. What do you mean? Because I cut my hair I want to be boy?" . . . Sometimes my mom will still be like, "Can you try to look like a girl." And I'm like, "What do you mean?"

As students shared these accounts, they critiqued their family members for policing gender by saying things like "I don't see the problem" and asking things like "What do you mean?" In doing so, they moved away from family members who policed gender, whether it was their own, as in Terry's account, or that of their siblings, as in Carter's and Yanika's stories. They moved away from parental gender policing even when they themselves were not being policed or when they were even though they identified as cisgender. In doing so, they protected themselves from the potential damage such policing can cause.

Students also critiqued their families for their lack of knowledge of sexual and gender identities. Often parents thought their children's sexual identities were phases. According to Darby, who identified as cisgender, when she came out as gay to her mother, her mother assumed it was a phase. Darby said, "She was like, 'Oh, well, now that you go to that school, this is just, like, a fad. This is just, like, a popularity thing. You just want to be a part of it.'" She rejected her mom's understanding. Then, later, when found herself attracted to a boy, she told her mother, "'Oh, I think I like this boy.' She was like, 'Oh, I told you it was just a phase.'" Darby reported trying to explain to her mother, "'It is not just that I like one or the other. There is room in between to like both, or there are so many different spectrums than just black and white on this.' She was like, 'Oh, so what? You want to become a boy now, too?' I was like, 'Mom, you are being rude about it.' She does not—she is trying, but she does not really get that there is more than a black and white spectrum of it." Darby acknowledged that this was a "hard concept to grasp" for her mother, who asked, "Well, what is that called?" to which Darby replied, "Read a book, Mom." Darby critiqued her mother for her lack of knowledge about sexual identities, particularly *her* sexual identity, which, by the way, was not bisexual or pansexual but rather "unidentified" because she "just like[s] who [she] like[s]." Her critique was evident when she said, about her mother, "She does not really get" it and when she told her to "read a book." With such comments, Darby moved away from her mother and what she experienced as her mother's ignorance, thus protecting herself from it.

Katherine, who identified as bisexual and white, also critiqued her parents for their ignorance with respect to sexual identities. She said,

> Sometimes [my parents] say things that kind of are insulting to me or like weird, like almost homophobic without realizing it, you know? . . . So it's not like they're doing it on purpose. But I remember really clearly, I came home and I was chilling on the couch, watching TV, [and talking about Mac and Joan], and my parents were in the room. They were like, "You know what? You need some straight friends." I got mad too because I was like, "I don't need straight friends. Like, that's not what I'm looking for in a friend; it doesn't matter to me if you're an LGBT or straight." Like, it shouldn't matter, but they got so mad; they're like, "You need to do things like go to straight bars."

At this point, everyone in the class started laughing. I said, sarcastically, "You'll never find a man if you don't have any straight friends," and I asked, "Are they at all concerned that you'd be going to bars?" And Yanika suggested that was not what "normal parents" would tell their kids to do. Here, Katherine certainly provided an effective example of how her parents were sometimes ignorantly and passionately homophobic. Her example was so effective that others in the class joined Katherine in her critique.

Katherine, months later, described her parents as not only ignorant but actively dismissive, particularly of her bisexual identity. She told the

Moving with Respect to Families | 139

class about coming out to them, about explaining that it was not a phase and that she wanted to be respected as bisexual. She then explained their reaction:

> KATHERINE: And they do this thing where parents are like, "Oh, okay," you know? And they kind of just sweep it aside like, "Oh, okay. Sure."

> ANN: Pat you on the head a little?

> KATHERINE: Yeah, and say, "Oh, you silly teenager, you." And they kind of, you know, like, let it go, but, you know, I'll say things like, "Oh, I think she's really attractive," and my mom will be like, "Oh, yeah. Well, she's a woman to look up to and, you know, to respect."

> DR. B.: She just reframes in a way that works for her, yeah.

> KATHERINE: Right, you know, I'm just admiring her because I think she is a strong woman, not because I think she's, you know—I don't want to be shallow, but I think she's beautiful and I think she has a nice personality and I think I would, you know, like, date her. And my parents will kind of get kind of quiet when I say, "Oh, I think she's really pretty. You know, I would love to date her," and my parents get really quiet. Whenever I say it about a guy, my mom's like, "Oh, yeah, he's cute!" and I'm like, you know, it doesn't really match, so I think they're trying to kind of make sense of it in a way, that I'm not really bisexual and I'm just confusing my feelings with admiring women.

> DR. B.: Yeah, that's what it sounds like.

> KATHERINE: It's kind of distancing—this refusal to kind of accept it and try to put it on something else. It really gets on my nerves.

Here, Katherine explicitly named the movement away from her parents as they refused to accept her sexual identity. Katherine's movement away is not solely of her own doing; by refusing to accept her, her parents push her away from them.

Ann, who identified as homoromantic, cis, and white, immediately connected to Katherine's story, saying, "I think there's a big, big difference between accepting *despite* and accepting *because*." I thought I heard the connection, but I wasn't sure, so I asked her to say more. She referred to herself "as the official gay delegation in [her] family," and said,

> The thing is, there are people who can accept you, but they're not going to actually care about that part of you. It's the whole "Love the sinner, hate the sin" thing, which I totally supported at a point in my life, when I had no idea. I had some idea, but I was terrified of it—to acknowledge my own homoromantic-ness. And there's this feeling that if you accept them despite of it, it's going to change someday. Like, if you can just love them hard enough, you'll love the gay away. And then "accepting because" is where you look at this person and you look at all of them and you go, "Okay, I love you *because* of who you are, not *despite* who you are." I think before I acknowledged myself—exactly how queer I am—I didn't realize what a huge part of someone's identity it is. . . . So, it sort of made sense to me that you could love someone despite—you really can't.

Ann had clearly moved on the issue; she had moved away from homophobic ideas. Similarly, in September, students laughed with Katherine about her parents, but later, in December, Ann responded personally and somberly. Again, she moved. In both September and December, Katherine moved farther away from her parents, not alone but with her classmates. Across these accounts, students' awareness that their understandings of gender and sexuality were less finite than those of their family members distanced them from those family members, at least during these moments in time. This distancing limited future opportunities for connecting with family.

Understanding Parents

After Katherine expressed her frustration with Arin's mom for not listening to her child before he became suicidal, discussed above, Vic, who identified as lesbian, cis, and Black, explained, drawing on a lesson her mother taught her. She said,

> My mom explained this to me, a couple of years ago or something like that, how like, when most people have kids, they judge how their kids are going to be. Like if you hear you're going to have a girl, you're like, "I'm going to do this; I get to dress her up like [indecipherable]" and stuff like that, and that's probably what his mom had envisioned for him when like he was born as a girl. So like, it's kind of like really traumatic on the parent part, because [indecipherable], "I really love having a young girl, but, like, I need to like get used to this," because you know, it's like, now you [indecipherable]; it's like, "If you don't listen to me, I'm going to die." And that's probably how she felt, so it's just like really—it was really emotional.

Here, Vic moved toward parents of trans kids with the help of her mother. I affirmed Vic's account, saying, "You do hear parents talk about going through a period of mourning or loss. I have to give up my son in order to raise my daughter. Instead of just being, I love my child." Katherine had no patience for this, saying, "Your child is your child. It shouldn't matter. Male or female, she's still your child. I mean, you love them, but it's like, mourning? . . . I feel like it's too much. Too much." Others, however, seemed to respect Arin's patience with his mother's grief as he transitioned. I had expressed appreciation that Arin "showed that he wasn't just resentful. But that he could see her love for him in those struggles" with his transition, and Mac pointed to a particular place in the book to illustrate that:

> It was also kind of like that when he was going in to get his top surgery, chilling in [indecipherable] where—she was saying, or, like, thinking, and he didn't want to, like, talk about how stoked he was to finally have top surgery . . . he's like, you know, "I'm going to let her think about it because this is kind of like the final step. Almost. And, like, this real for her, so I don't want to gloat in her face about how excited I am while she's kind of, like, grieving."

Then Vic said, "Like, he was like really, really, like, understanding of his mom." Similarly, Mac noted that Arin was patient with his mother when he said "I got to give her time," and Mac respected that "a lot." Although I would not argue that Mac and Vic understood the mother's grief, they did respect and maybe even admire *Arin's* ability to understand his mother's grief. Even so, by reflecting on the potential grief of parents of trans children, Vic moved closer to those parents, whereas Katherine moved farther away from them. Vic was opening the possibilities of connection, while Katherine was conveying an intolerance for transphobia.

Students did seem to understand, however, parents' fear, and in doing so they moved closer to them. When the third-semester class was reading and discussing *Beyond Magenta*, which I describe in chapter 2, the students talked about Christina, who is a trans Latina featured in the book. Khalil, who was gay, embodied gender expansiveness, and identified as multiracial, expressed frustration that Christina's mom "wants Christina to keep her chin down." He says, "If she keeps her chin up, it makes her feel more comfortable and confident. . . . But if she had to keep her chin down it makes her look like she's not comfortable with being who she is." He acknowledged that "she wanted her to hide her Adam's apple" but was still worried about the impact on Christina. Kristy, however, worked to consider Christina's mother's point of view, not only with respect to Christina as a trans woman but also with respect to Christina's brother, who is gay. She said,

> She's so afraid, like—I don't even think it's that they're gay or transsexual. It's that they can be hurt and that someone else who's going to find out is going to hurt them. And I think that's like what a lot of the moms' motives are. She may have had a problem with it at the beginning, but like I think another part of it really was that a lot of people didn't agree with it at the time, so she was afraid that her kids were going to walk out the door and get, like, beat up or something, like how Christina was punched in the face. And I think, like, that honestly was what caused a lot of her, like, reactions most of the time.

Kristy understood the mother's fear when reading about it in *Beyond Magenta* and was able to articulate it to the class. In understanding Christina's mother's fear, she moved closer to her. By reflecting on the potential grief of parents of trans children, Kristy moved closer to those parents, whereas Khalil moved farther away from them, again show a tension between the desire to connect and the refusal to tolerate transphobia.

There were also times when students worked to understand their own parents' fear, but in the case of their own parents this reflection helped them move closer to them. In an interview just weeks before Khalil critiqued Christina's mother, he defended his mother for similar actions.

> KHALIL: I finally became comfortable. I'm like, "Look, I'm gonna wear skinny jeans, I'm gonna have mascara on." . . . I decided just do my full face and go downstairs to my mom and be like, "Look." . . . She's like, "You're almost eighteen"; I was like, "I know, I have less than a month now." So she was like, "You do whatever you want," and then she told me, "Don't wear it on the [local public] bus."
>
> DR. B.: What do you think that's about?
>
> KHALIL: She don't want nobody hurting me, and I was like, "Okay," and so I now—
>
> DR. B.: She wants you to be safe. . . .
>
> KHALIL: —Yeah. So she gave me pepper spray, so I have that on me at all times.

Here, Khalil's mother moved closer to him by recognizing and accommodating his independence, but Khalil also moved closer to her by recognizing and accommodating her concern. Thus, when it came to his own parent, Khalil prioritized moving closer and opening up possibilities of connection.

As the only parent in the room, I sometimes provoked such movement toward parents, including of me toward my own. In one of our conversations about Arin Andrews and Katie Rain Hill, I said, "There's an issue around safety, too. So like, I know, and this was a long time ago, I came out—or the year after was the year Matthew Shepard was murdered, and so for my mom, well she was very conservative, and so she had all sorts of issues, but, but, to also be like, 'I am afraid you're going to get hurt. I want you to have an easy life; this is going be a harder life.'" After I shared this, several students told stories about their parents' concern for their safety as queer youth. Katherine, for example, acknowledged that when she was "hanging out with [Mac]," her parents were "so worried that since . . . I was around them, and we were dating, and we're not a straight couple, that, you know, I'm going to be targeted for a hate crime. They were just, they were so [indecipherable], so cautious." Katherine was annoyed, as indicated by her next statement: "and like, to me, my parents were just so hyperfocused on that one thing." Still, she moved closer to her parents as she noted their worry. Thus, like Khalil, Katherine prioritized moving closer and opening up possibilities of connection when in relation to her own parents.

Similarly, Vic, who identified as gay, said, "Whenever I go out on dates . . . before I walk out the door, [my mom is] always like, 'No holding hands. No, like, [indecipherable], no kissing,' and stuff like that." Vic, like Katherine, also expressed her annoyance, saying, "She thinks I'm like going to like make out in public. I'm not that kind of kid." She went on to say, however, "I can understand where they come from, I guess. But my mom thinks—my mom sees the world very negatively; she's like kind of negative. So I think that's why she's so scared about everything." According to Yanika, her father seemed to share the same kind of concern for Yanika's sister when she started dating a woman, but instead of telling her not to display affection publicly he said, "All right, time to teach you how to box." In this way, Yanika's father encouraged his daughter not to hide herself from homophobes but to be able to defend herself against them. Through sharing these stories, students worked to understand their own parents and, in doing so, moved themselves and one another closer to them.

As students worked to understand parents represented in the books we read and discussed together, they would sometimes pull closer to them and other times push farther away from them, but when it came to working to understand their own parents students were much more likely to pull closer to them, and sometimes, particularly in the case of Khalil, this pulling closer also provoked parents to pull closer to their children as well. As a parent myself, this pulling closer was something I tended to encourage. Such movement opened up a future of possible encounters in which students could maintain their dignity in their identities and share intimate relationships with their parents, simultaneously.

Appreciating Parents

Students also moved closer to parents—both in literature and in their lives—by appreciating when they were kind, loving, affirming, open to learning about their children, and standing up for them. In the second-semester class, for example, we had read the first section of *Aristotle and Dante Discover the Secrets of the Universe* (Sáenz, 2012) and were discussing the following journal prompt: "Select a character. Describe his/her personality. Point to the places in the novel that let you know this is his/her personality."[1] Several students wrote about parents. Carter, for example, wrote about Dante's father, who is an academic. She described him as "kind understanding honest thoughtful." She gave examples from the book of each of these traits and then said, "He seems really chill. Really nice." Ann and Yanika wrote about Ari's mother, who is a teacher. Ann said, "She's primarily driven by love for her son." Yanika said, "Lily seems like just [a] very loving mother." Being kind and loving were qualities that, of course, drew students to parents, at least to those in the novel *Aristotle and Dante Discover the Secrets of the Universe*.

Students also valued when parents explicitly affirmed their children. For example, when we were talking about Arin's mother learning to affirm him in *Some Assembly Required* (Andrews, 2014), Hilary said, "I just want to, like, point something out. It was, like, my favorite part . . . when his mom, like, finally, like—was like 100 percent, I feel like, on it, because she was like taking him to, like, counseling and, like, was finally letting him get his hair cut, and like right after he got his hair cut, like he, she let him, like, change his name. I thought that was really, like, sweet of him—I mean, of her—to do that." That this was Hilary's "favorite part" of the book strikes me as important. This was clear movement toward Arin's mother, particularly since there was so much ire toward her earlier. Yanika, too, said her "favorite part" of *If You Could Be Mine* (Farizan, 2013) was when the Sahar's father starts getting treatment for his depression and "starts coming back." Neither of these "favorite parts" were momentous ones in their respective books, but seeing parents affirm and support their children mattered to some students, resulting in them moving closer to those parents.

Also of significance were the times when parents stuck up for their children. We talked about this in the third semester in relation to Christina's story in *Beyond Magenta*. Christina has been "punched . . . in the face" (Kuklin, 2014, p. 68), and her mother approached a group of men

---

1. If I were writing this prompt now, I would use "their" instead of "his/her," as supported by the National Council of Teachers of English's *Statement on Gender and Language* (DesPrez et al., 2018).

who she believed included the one who assaulted her daughter, and she walked right up to him and "told him off" (p. 68). Ultimately the man confesses, and his friends tell her, "'Don't worry ma'am. From now on, we're going to have respect for her. We're going to watch out for her'" (Kuklin, 2014, p. 68). Khalil said, "I feel like everybody could relate to the story, whether you're trans, gay, or not, because this part, her mom went to go defend her not knowing what could happen, she still did it anyway." Students valued loving and affirming parents in the books we read and discussed, and they also valued parents who stood up for their children. This valuing resulted in their moving closer to these parents.

Students appreciated the same efforts in their own parents. One way that they reported their parents showed they cared was by learning from them. Mac, for example, said that their parents had "never been exposed to anyone who's transgender," so they try to model appropriate behavior for their parents, and when their parents ask about why Mac does what they do, Mac answers their questions. They reported,

> When I talk about my gender-fluid friends and I say "they," they're like, "Wait, they?" And I'm like, "Yeah, they. That's, like, a pronoun that they use." And especially my mom, she's like, "That doesn't make sense because *they* is not a pronoun." And I'm like, "Mom, it is. You don't have to understand. You just have to, like, accept it and use the right pronoun, even if you [don't] understand. Just have enough respect to use the right pronoun." And she tries. She does. Like, when my friends come over, she tries to use the pronouns that, you know, they want. She'll ask.

Here, Mac indicated that they valued their mother trying to be respectful to their gender-fluid friends, whether or not she understood. Hilary also talked about teaching her parent to be respectful were she to have "a transgender friend come over." She explained that she would "tell him what the right pronouns are," but she worried that he would "slip up a lot." She said she would "give him a death look" until he modified his behavior. Although Mac told their story as if based on actual events from the past and Hilary told hers based on hypothetical events in the future, both represented their parents as people with whom they can talk and whom they can even educate. As such, they pulled their parents closer to them as they taught or imagined teaching them to be respectful of trans people, particularly their friends.

Students further valued when their parents' learning was followed by affirmation. Khalil told stories about his mother and father not "really understanding everything" but eventually his mother "help[ing him] through it" and his "biggest supporters" being his sister; stepfather, whom he calls Dad; and best friends. His dad supported him by talking explicitly about his experience of Khalil's gender expressions. Khalil said, "Just the other day, my dad was like, 'What do you go by? Because me and your mom was talking about this the other night and . . . I don't know what to call you, and I don't want to make a mistake.'" By explicitly asking Khalil about his gender pronouns and stating that he did not want to "make a mistake," Khalil's dad showed his support of him. Also, Khalil's parents affirmed him through their support of a drag performance. Khalil reported that his mom attended his performance and was really proud of him. Jenna said, "She was in the crowd, she was going wild." Khalil agreed, "Yeah she was a mess." His dad could not attend, but, after the event, Khalil said, "He was like, 'I heard about the drag show, da-da-da-da-da'; he was all happy." That his parents' support was of consequence to him was evident when he said, in the same interview, "Well, I'm taking my stepdad's last name." This was a clear indication of Khalil moving closer to his parents.

Just as students appreciated when parents in the books we read and discussed stood up for their kids, they valued when their own parents stood up for them. In fact, when Khalil praised Christina's mother for standing up for Christina in *Beyond Magenta*, Delilah said this scene reminded her of her mom, and she proudly told a story about her mom confronting the mother of a girl who started a fight with Delilah. Similarly, as you will recall from the previous chapter, Khalil talked about when his family started going to a church that they really liked. He said, "When I first went there, I was gay but I wasn't fully out to everybody." His family knew, but the church leaders did not. Because he "loved it" and because he was a "little church boy," he decided "to keep [his] secret in." He described the pastor as like a "grandfather to me," and he said he "loved" the pastor's wife, but then the pastor's wife started "trying to take the demons out of [him]." According to Khalil, she said, "If you're going to still contribute to this lifestyle, you can't be here." So he said to himself, "I can't do this." Then he told his mother about it, and "she was just like, 'we're going to stop going there because I'm not going to have somebody belittle my son all the time.'" In these parents' acts of standing up for their children, as reported in our class discussions, parents moved closer to their children and their children moved closer to their parents, achieving a sort of familial intimacy, at least for particular moments in time. These moments opened up the possibility of future moments in time in which LGBTQ+ and ally youth could have their identities and values not only recognized but honored and protected by their parents, bringing them closer together through love and respect.

Ethical Movement with
Respect to Families in Classroom Encounters

There were parents who would not allow their children to be in the class; or, even if they let them take the class, they would not allow them to participate in this study; or, even if they let them participate, they worried that I was essentially trying to recruit them into being gay. But the sexual and gender identities of the students did not hinge on our reading and discussion of LGBTQ+-themed literature. However, their ability to talk with their families about these identities and to understand their parents' concerns about these identities often did increase, and often with my encouragement. Thus, our reading and discussion of LGBTQ+-inclusive literature moved students closer to their parents and families, at least in some moments in time.

Sometimes parents pushed their children away from them, like Bruce in *Fun Home*. Other times young people moved themselves away from parents and family members who were ignorant about their sexual and gender identities, dismissed them, or failed to respect them or take them seriously. They also moved away from parents and family members who policed their gender or loved them *despite* who they were rather than because of who they were. Even so, students also talked about really trying to understand parents in literature and in their lives who mourned for the idea of who they thought their children would be and who deeply feared their children would be hurt for who they actually were. This moved students closer to parents, as did when they experienced parents—again in literature and in their lives—loving their children, learning about their children, affirming them, and standing up for them.

Whether students moved toward parents or away from them is not an indication of whether the encounters were ethical. I understand both the movement away from parents and the movement toward parents as ethical because the young people were listening, paying attention, taking responsibility, and asserting themselves while they moved. They moved away from parents to protect themselves; they moved toward parents to connect with them. Sometimes they moved back and forth. Such movement might seem counterproductive, but it's not; it's complicated, to be sure, but movement in both directions was needed, and is needed, to make the familial relationships both respectful of the young people's identities and values and loving between parents and children. Such respect and love are imperative for the familial relationships to be ethical. And the movement required to make the familial relationships ethical demanded great agility, particularly from the young people.

Chapter 6

Moving, (For)Giving, and Ethical Classroom Encounters

As I read and reread the conversations I had selected for transcription and examined and reexamined the encounters I had identified as pertinent to this study, I started to notice that I often referenced forgiveness. For example, when I was trying to get students to understand that Levithan's (2009) "A Word from the Nearly Distant Past" was about, in part, the AIDS epidemic, and as I thought, wrongly, that they were getting close to making the connection, Kristy said, "This was kind of [indecipherable], but, like, um, I'm going to say it wrong if I say it," and I said, "That's okay. We forgive you." Here, I was trying to encourage her to get us closer to what I understood as the point of the story, but in doing so I spoke not only for myself but for the class, saying "we" would forgive whatever it was Kristy would say, not even knowing whether it was forgivable and, if so, for whom.

Another time, we were talking about indicators of Kid's sex in Brezenhoff's (2011) *Brooklyn, Burning*, and Rhys said, "What about height? *He* said, *the thing* said—sorry, that was terrible" (emphases are mine). In doing so, they turned a human, Kid, into an object, or "thing." I corrected and excused Rhys by saying, "That's okay. You mean *Kid* said. . . . It's okay. We're going to forgive each other." Thus, I, a cisgender person, forgave Rhys for their transphobic language, which was decidedly inappropriate. Further, I again spoke not only for myself but for the class. I implicitly demanded that students in my class, even trans kids, forgive transphobic language. It matters that during this semester and in this class, Rhys was experimenting with gender and that they identified their older brother

151

as trans, but that does not give me the right to forgive them on behalf of others.

In another situation, I again, as with Rhys, tried to forgive transphobia, something I just cannot do as a cisgender person. Katherine was explaining how her father was struggling to call one of Katherine's friends by the correct name and pronouns since his transition. She said he was trying but not always succeeding. She sympathized with him, saying, "I would, you know, use the wrong [pronoun], and then I'd be really upset with myself; I'm like, kind of disappointed. But that's kind of what's happening to [my father] now." I replied saying, "I think that's hard for people because the heteronormative way of being is we know the pronouns to use and we just assume and use them. Um, and I think it's hard for people and that we forgive one another, like that's how we move forward is that we mess up and we forgive one another and we move on." This time, "we" represented people beyond the classroom. The "we" could be almost anyone. In fact, I suggest the "we" in this context is people, *all* people. And I say that "we" mess up and forgive, bypassing the steps of apologizing and trying to do better on one hand, and bypassing the steps of healing on the other hand—the hand which includes trans people in particular.

In addition to my demanding that the whole class forgive or that all people forgive, there was a situation in which I insisted a single student forgive others, including those beyond the class. Darby was sharing her frustration with people who did not call her by her correct name or use her chosen name during times when she elected to use her middle name, Margaret, or variations of it like Maggie, Peg, or Peggy or selected an alternative name, like Christine. She was frustrated by not being called by her chosen names in the same way she was frustrated by how people reacted when she came out as straight after having come out as lesbian. She said that people were like, "You were a lesbian first. Nothing beyond that matters." I responded saying, "I think that is about people trying to make sense of people. You know the complexities and nuances of yourself in a way that other people are never going to have full access to. In some ways, I think there has got to be some forgiveness there. You cannot expect people to be as invested in your wholeness as you are." In effect, I told Darby that she needed to forgive those who were not respectful of her identities. When I reflect on my assumptions regarding forgiveness and my demands for it, I regret them.

Yanika, though, encouraged students to forgive one another in ways that students had not forgiven one of the people we had read and discussed: Nat. In *Beyond Magenta*, Nat writes, "Usually I don't like to use labels, but if I did, I would say I was gender queer, gender neutral, or simply queer. Intersex is another way I can identify myself" (Kuklin, 2014, p. 121). Students had critiqued several things about Nat's story, including their use of the word "normal" to describe someone who is cisgender. Yanika pointed out that Nat was very open and that if we were all that open, we would also probably say some things that could be critiqued. She said, "I'm just thinking we're all capable of doing that, and like making like stupid comments. And maybe they go back and read it and go, 'Wait, I didn't mean it like that.' . . . I just don't want that to take away from the story, because it did teach me a lot." Thus, Yanika acknowledged the critiques her classmates were making but then also reminded them of their and her own capacity to make errors and not to allow such errors to interrupt the lessons they offered one another. Implicitly, she asked her classmates to forgive Nat and one another, or maybe she asked that they give (Ahmed, 2000).

I made the connection both to students' upcoming memoir writing and to my own experience as a writer. In terms of students' memoirs, I said, "Yes, yes. I love that you brought that comment up, because next week we'll start writing our own memoirs. So we need to kind of *give* each other the space that we need to kind of make mistakes and learn from them—so that's a great comment." Notice that I used the word *give* rather than *forgive*. I went on, then, to connect to my own experience as a writer:

And [that comment] is really resonating with me, because last night, my university class read an article that I had written. And I used the term—and I used a term that I know better [than] to use—I know not to use now. But I didn't then. So when I read it, I was like—I used "transgendered" with the *-ed* at the end. Which, when you describe someone, you say somebody is "transgender," not transgendered. But I didn't know that then. And it got published. And . . . people . . . read that mistake of mine. It was just an awful feeling. I just read it—and every copy I have, I have to, like, scratch the *-ed* off. Like, "I promise I didn't mean that."

Here, I identified with how Yanika was imagining Nat to feel and applied that imagining to how her classmates and she might feel when they shared their memoirs by telling my own story of feeling that way. Then, I brought her comment back to our class. I said, "Next week when we start writing our own memoirs, just know that we will *forgive* one another for our mistakes, and we'll help one another on things that make us uncomfortable." Again, I went back to demanding forgiveness. I do not mean to suggest that forgiving is an inherently bad thing to do. The problem in these cases was that I—as a teacher and therefore the person in a position of authority in this context—demanded that students forgive others when those others were directly violating identities they had worked hard to own.

There were other times, though, when I invited students to reflect on the possibility of forgiveness by talking about it in more detail. In one case, I turned the gaze back to myself, showing myself both forgiving and being forgiven. Students had written and were sharing journal entries in response to this prompt: "Write about an event in your life that significantly changed the way you view and/or do things." Cobalt asked, "What's *your* response to that?" I tried to explain how my best friend from high school's cancer diagnosis, which was four years prior to this conversation, changed the way we interacted between then and his death, which was two years prior to this conversation. I shared that we had made a lot of mistakes with each other over the almost three decades we were friends and that those mistakes taught us "to forgive each other a lot, and I think it's because of learning how to do that pretty early on, we had a lifetime of that. His lifetime of that, together." Here, I made explicit how our past years of complicated friendship allowed the encounter in which he shared his diagnosis with me to happen and also how that encounter shaped the months that followed. This act aligns with Ahmed's (2000) suggestion that we ask, "What made [an] encounter possible (historicity), but also what does it make possible, what futures might it open up?" (p. 145) In this classroom encounter, the "future" I referenced was the time between my friend's diagnosis and death, but the classroom encounter was also a part of the "future" opened up by his diagnosis. In that, Sherry picked up on the notion of forgiveness in friendships. She said, "That's pretty much everyone though," and I agreed. Thus, when I shared about my experiences with forgiveness, Sherry, at least, aligned herself and others with those experiences. This was quite different from my demanding forgiveness from her and others.

There were also times when I encouraged students to forgive one another in abstract terms. For example, when we were discussing Sáenz's (2012) *Aristotle and Dante Discover the Secrets of the Universe*, we talked about how people's experiences, or lack thereof, shaped their understanding of queer people. I said, "It's one of the reasons I want us to listen to each other with forgiveness, is we all have different sets of experiences that we bring together, and if we are constantly saying 'this is a stupid thing you've said'—we need to be able to say when things hurt us, but to frame it in stupidity worries me, whereas to frame it as 'I have something to offer you' feels more loving to me, and also is just more productive." Although I still focused on forgiveness, I offered a rationale for forgiveness and described it as a desire rather than demanding it from others for others. It feels more like giving than forgiving.

In another encounter, I did something similar. We were talking about trigger warnings with respect to the short stories students were writing and preparing to share with the class. I was conflicted about trigger warnings, mostly because I was hearing a call for them when stories made them uncomfortable rather than when they triggered PTSD, for example, and I was trying to consider alternatives with students. I said,

> Maybe we could be in conversation with one another about what we're writing, and just test each other's limits and see, um. Another thing I'd say about lines is that I think most of our, most of us have lines that change all of the time. You know? And that, so, some days I am more tolerant of some things than other days, and that, my lines just aren't the same. Even across the hour of class they might change depending on what's happened in the class. So, don't, let's uh, acknowledge that about one another. Don't forgive, but just understand that about one another, I guess. Does that feel like an okay way of moving forward?

I stepped a bit away from forgiveness, here. I explained that I wanted understanding from students, but I hedged. I started with "maybe" and ended with a question about whether my suggestion would work. Even when I sounded like I was demanding, saying, "Don't forgive, but just understand," I hedged by finishing the sentence with "I guess." Overall, there was a softer tone than when I assumed or demanded that students be forgiving. But still, underneath it all was the idea of forgiveness, and under that was the idea of giving.

Sometimes, however, students showed no inclination to forgive or to be forgiven. This was evident in an encounter where students were preparing to write memoirs, which led to a discussion of religion and empathy. Mac then told a story about their ex-boyfriend, whom Mac identified as trans. When they were dating, they went to a cookout at Mac's then-boyfriend's grandmother's house, and his aunt, whom Mac described as "really, really religious, like 'you're going to hell' kind of religious," came up to them while they were sitting on the couch, not "being really super affectionate," and, according to Mac, "she yelled at us, like, 'Don't bring that kind of personality into this house.'" Mac said the aunt "went on a rant" and then they "had to leave." Mac and their boyfriend at the time chose to get close to the boyfriend's family, and the encounter was hostile; it was not at all ethical. Mac said, "And it really made me upset, because—and she had the nerve to, like, hug us afterwards, and I'm like, 'Okay, goodbye. Goodbye.' But, you know, I wasn't going to like flip out or anything because it wasn't my family." Mac went on to say, though, that it was "really sad, because it wasn't the 'I love you, but you're going to hell.' It was the 'You're going to hell; I don't want you around' kind of thing. . . . I'm not saying that, 'I love you, but you're going to hell' kind of thing is okay, but it's like, you should feel love. But it's not okay, because it's not. It's not okay." In this situation, Mac offered no evidence of forgiveness and no one in the class verbalized any indication that they should forgive the ex-boyfriend's aunt. Rather, they pushed away from the hostility they experienced.

Sometimes students seemed to want to forgive, perhaps felt like they should, but simply could not do so. For example, in Carter's memoir, she shared how connected she was with her father until he left the family. She said that she "got down on [her] knees, crying and begging and pleading for [him] to stay." He asked her to go with him, but she could not. She said, "I didn't understand why you would leave us. Even now, I don't." And, finally, she read, "The little girl that lives within me wants to forgive you, but the woman I am now just won't let her." Here, Carter considers forgiving, perhaps even tries to forgive her father but cannot, at least not in this moment in time, when he moved away from her.

Other times students seemed to want to forgive, perhaps felt like they should, and moved in that direction. For example, in Mac's introductory interview, they told me about how horribly their brother treated them. He struggled with internalized homophobia and externalized this onto Mac. They said, "I don't hate him anymore because he's made, like, really large steps to, like, change our relationship . . . so our relationship has gotten better, and it's because I've been so open; if I decided to hold a grudge against him, then we wouldn't be where we are. . . . I just got to, I've, it's hard to forgive him because he hasn't really addressed it, but I've been trying to, not forget, just move on, you know, 'cause I'm becoming an adult, he's an adult." Here Mac seemed to think they should forgive their brother because they are both maturing. Mac saw that both of them were trying in different ways, but forgiving was hard for Mac. They were trying, instead, to "just move on." In this way, we see some give between Mac and their brother—give not evident between Mac and their ex-boyfriend's aunt and not yet evident between Carter and her father. A decision Mac made, and perhaps their brother made too, to "move on" toward a "better" relationship. For as much as I went on about forgiveness, I can't say that I wanted Mac to forgive their ex-boyfriend's aunt or even for Carter to forgive her father or Mac their brother. That seemed to be asking a lot. Maybe too much.

Giving

Giving, too, is asking a lot, but not too much, maybe. Giving is what is necessary, according to Ahmed (2000), for people to get close enough to one another in an encounter to make it an ethical encounter. I reference give between Mac and their brother above and, before that, in what Yanika and I asked for from classmates as they responded to interviews and memoirs, but it is worth looking more closely at some classroom encounters to consider what give might look like.

The day after the panel to discuss trans issues in the fall of 2015, we were debriefing in class, and Vic and Yanika, both cisgender students, talked about how they try to get people's pronouns right but sometimes they "slip up" when they knew the people before their transition. Mac replied first, as someone in their situation. You might recall from chapter 2 that they said, "I find that it's a lot easier to do it, like—so, when my ex first came out to me as trans, it was a lot easier to switch the pronouns to, like, what he wanted over the text. And then when I talked to him, I've accidently slipped up, and then like, 'I have got to get better.' Because, like, over text you can just delete the message and be like, 'Oh wait, that's not right,' and then fix it. But when you're speaking it just comes out." Then, almost immediately, they replied as a trans person:

> MAC: So I—I kind of understand. And it's like—you slip up; you're human. As long as you know that it was mistake and that you try, I feel like that's what counts. Like, it's still frustrating; that's okay.

> DR. BLACKBURN: What I heard on the panel was that it hurts.

> MAC: It does.

In this interaction, Mac affirmed people for trying without denying the frustration and pain caused by the times that people get pronouns wrong. Again, we see Mac giving, regardless of whether they were forgiving, which is perhaps irrelevant. Instead, they were giving.

In the fall of 2015, we were reading and discussing Cameron's story in *Beyond Magenta* (Kuklin, 2014). In their story, Cameron, who is white and queer, calls for all minoritized people to advocate for one another. Some students talked about how this might be an ideal but it is not realistic since there is so much diversity within any community of people and even more across various communities. In exploring the real and ideal divide, Vic, who was Black and gay, stated that there are "gay people who are racist" and "Black people . . . or like [racial] minorities in general . . . [who] are homophobic." While students recognized this as reality, some expressed a desire for things to be different. Ann, who was white and homoromantic, said, "Just because . . . people of marginalized groups, they don't automatically feel any empathy for people from other marginalized groups, doesn't mean they shouldn't." Not all students, however, shared such an ideal:

> YANIKA: I think that that assumption is unfair to make. And it's—for me, it doesn't make sense, because like, okay, if you can have a room full of, like, all white people, and they're not—not everybody's able to like each other. So even people that are in the same category or having, like, the same job or, like, the same struggles aren't going to like each other even though they're, like, inside the same group and they do, like, experience similar things, obviously not everybody gets along.

So then, to stretch—to take that a step further and say that people that are in, like—

Dr. B.: Across different marginalized groups.

Yanika: Yeah, just because they are like, um, not like the norm or whatever, that they're automatically going to get along and they're automatically going to understand each other. It's just kind of like, where did you get that from? Kind of—it just doesn't make sense to me.

Yanika's ideal was not Ann's. Nor was it Carter's. I tried to name the conflict with Carter, saying, "So you and [Yanika] are totally disagreeing, is that correct?" Carter seemed caught off guard. I explained why I named what I understood as opposing viewpoints: "If you're finding each other's viewpoints really, um, hard to get, like, it's good to talk about that. Not so that anybody can convince anybody of anything differently, but just, like, to understand one another better. Right? Let's keep thinking, keep thinking about it." Here, I was encouraging students to talk with each other across differences, to try to understand one another, to give rather than give in or give up.

Mac, though, explained that giving is "the hardest part of being a human." They said, "It's really hard to see from someone else's view, which I think is amazing if you can. I always try to. And it's hard." I replied, "It's work. Right?" and they said, "It is, and it's like, I always try, but it's like, sometimes it doesn't work, sometimes it does." Carter agreed with Mac; she said,

I just highly agree with you. . . . I try to be, like, as open as possible about things. I mean, I of course still have my own personal opinions and am like, 'Yeah, this is what I personally believe,' but when someone wants to offer, like, a different view about it, I try to the best of my ability, especially if I've, like, already assessed that situation or that thought process and just don't agree with it, but like when people do offer their opinions, I do listen to them, and I, like, try to understand, like, where they're coming from. What possibly, like, what could possibly, like, what possibly could they have gone through that they have that personal opinion about that certain subject, so.

Yanika said, "I feel like it also takes a really special kind of person . . . it's not common. Like you just don't see it in everybody. . . . They just have this mind-blowing ability to be so, like, empathetic." Through talking about "see[ing] from someone else's point of view," in Mac's words, and by being "as open as possible," "try[ing] to the best of my ability," and "listen[ing]," in Carter's words, students talked about giving. They talked about it as "hard" but also as "amazing," "special," and "mind-blowing." And we see it in Mac's words in class the morning after the trans panel as well as in careful, thoughtful, and respectful conflict. We see giving—not giving in, not giving up, and not forgiving. We see giving.

Ethical Encounters

It is this give that is the crux of ethical encounters. Ahmed (2000) says, "In my notion of ethical encounters, hearing does not take place in my ear, or in yours, but in between our mouths and our ears, in the very proximity and multiplicity of this encounter." (p. 158). That is to say, ethical encounters, like all encounters, are constructed socially, they are constructed among people, places, and times with histories and futures, but ethical encounters "kee[p] alive the circuit between mouths, ears, and skin" by relying on "the act of getting closer" (Ahmed, 2000, p. 158). But sometimes, as you will recall from chapter 1, a firm stance is more ethical than movement, and sometimes, as you will recall from chapter 5, movement away is more ethical than moving toward. Ethical encounters, though, demand movement toward, otherwise we do not encounter one another. Ahmed (2000) argues that "it is through getting closer . . . that the impossibility of pure proximity can be put to work, or made to work" (p. 157). And this is where giving comes in. According to Ahmed (2000), "one could not get close enough to have an ethical encounter" without "the very act of giving" (p. 150). In other words, in order to share ethical encounters, we must be close to one another; in order to move closer to one another, we must give, and to give is a gift.

But Ahmed is not naive. Such movement, the movement of getting closer, is complicated and challenging. She states that ethical encounters "always conceal as much as they reveal: they involve trauma, scars, wounds, and tears that are impossible to forget (they affect how we arrive or face each other, the encounter itself involves a form of remembering) *or* to present or to speak" (Ahmed, 2000, p. 158). That is to say, the histories of hurt that, in part, shape how we face one another are not explicitly shared with one another. They are there, but they are not always named or acknowledged. Ahmed (2000) asserts, "Communication [then] involves working with, 'that which fails to get across,' or that which is necessarily secret" (p. 155). This does not mean that those sharing ethical encounters should ignore those histories of hurt. In fact, Ahmed (2000) conceptualizes these histories of hurt as a "debt" and a "violence" and argues that a "gift cannot be given" (p. 152) without recognizing "the debts that are already accrued" (p. 154) and "responding to the violence" (p. 152). This means that giving requires taking responsibility.

She readily admits that taking responsibility is an "impossibility" (Ahmed, 2000, p. 148), but it is one worth striving for nonetheless. Such striving must also be "generous," which Ahmed (2000) conceptualizes as "ways of being with (or, more precisely, for) others" (p. 140) and as being "in a way which gives" (p. 149). In order to strive to be responsible and generous in encounters, she suggests "opening the encounter up," moving from "the now to the not yet" (Ahmed, 2000, p. 145). When she talks about ethical encounters, or better encounters, she means encounters that "may allow the other to exist beyond the grasp of the present" (Ahmed, 2000, p. 139). Here, I consider what it might look like to take responsibility for the past and to be generous toward a better—that is, more ethical—future.

In classroom encounters, when teachers and students move closer to one another, they must be agile, but they must also take responsibility for themselves and for their actions, including historical ones in which they are implicated. Further, they must be generous. This does not mean that they must forgive. Some things at some times in some places are quite simply not forgivable. And even if one person, like me, decides something is forgivable, they cannot impose this decision on someone else, like the students with whom I shared my class. People can only decide for themselves whether they forgive and, if they do, whom they forgive when and for what. But for teachers and students to share ethical encounters, they must give, even though giving is difficult.

Because giving is so challenging, so demanding, one might wonder why anyone would bother. Why not stay in one place? Why not stay in one's place? Why not choose ossification over agility? Vic considered these questions. She talked about how, from her point of view, older people tended to get stuck, whereas younger people, like Cameron, like herself, tended to move more, tended to be more agile. She described older people as "negative" and younger people as saying, " 'Why can't we all just get along?' Peace, love, all that stuff." She described the impact of these two ways of being in this way: "It's just like, when you're around a lot of negativity, it's kind of hard to start a revolution randomly, with no—when everybody else is like, 'I'm completely fine with the way things are.' You know, 'I'm completely fine not liking this person.' . . . Yeah, so it's kind of hard to be like 'Let's all love one another' when everybody else doesn't want to, too." If we think of this in terms of movement and forgiveness, Vic seems to think that people who are "fine not liking" an other are not only stuck but holding back those who are trying to move toward and share ethical encounters with one another. One is hindering if not preventing the revolutionary love of the other, of an other. It is the potential of this revolutionary love, the futures that ethical encounters might open up, in Ahmed's words, that makes giving worth the work and sometimes even worth the risk.

Conclusion

Moving and Giving toward Ethical Encounters

In part, this book strives to add to the conversation about young people reading, writing, and talking about LGBTQ+-themed literature by documenting those who do so in a school that strove to be queer-friendly and in a semester-long course for which students earned credit. It is a distinctive project in that way. Students were not assumed to be straight or cisgender, homophobic or transphobic. In these ways, it was like literacy groups in LGBTQ+ youth centers. Except the conversations included straight and cis people, as well, and the students earned credit for their work. LGBTQ+-themed literature was not taught as if it were taboo. It was not the focus of a singular lesson or embedded in a theme for a singular unit. It did not come up as an aside because one student braved initiating the topic. Rather, a wide range of LGBTQ+-themed literature was read, written about, and discussed, over an extended period of time. As such, the texts we shared were by and about diverse LGBTQ+ people. Not only were BT+ people included, when historically they have not been, but so too were multiple races, ethnicities, religions, and nationalities. As a result, the literature we shared could sometimes for some people assume the role of mirrors, other times for other people act as windows, and still other times act as doors (Botelho & Rudman, 2009; Sims Bishop, 1990). Further, some of this literature fell into Cart and Jenkins's (2006) categories of homosexual visibility and gay assimilation, but much of it fell into their queer community or queer consciousness category. In Adichie's (2009) words, we could avoid "the danger of a single story."[1]

---

1. I quote Adichie here although it gives me pause. Certainly this concept is one that I value, but I must acknowledge that in the years since her TED talk, Adichie has asserted that trans women are not women (Crockett, 2017) and therefore has been rightfully critiqued for being a trans-exclusionary radical feminist (TERF).

This does not, however, solve the dilemma articulated by Kumashiro (2001) about inclusion. Having the time and space to include more LGBTQ+-themed literature does not mean the course ever will or even can fully represent LGBTQ+ people or communities. There is always a point where individual people distinguish themselves from their communities and thus from one another. So, as a complement to inclusion, this study offers movement. While every person or community will never be included in any curriculum, curricula and pedagogy together can be used by teachers and students to provoke movement—movement in and out and around various communities to learn from, to learn with, and to teach one another. Movement depends on agility; movement is prevented by ossification. Encounters, ethical or otherwise, depend on movement. By exploring movement between, among, and within encounters and reflecting on related ethics, this study makes a theoretical contribution to this empirical body of literature.

Those of us in the LGBTQ+-themed literature courses used reading, writing, and talking about diverse literature to move across lines of difference defined in many ways, including but not limited to sexual identities, gender identities and expressions, racial identities, religious experiences, and familial experiences. With respect to lines of difference defined by sexual identities, some students stood firm, but most students moved, and not such in that they gave up one sexual identity for another but in how they experienced and understood their sexual identities, some moving toward more stability in these identities and others moving toward more fluidity. Here we saw evidence of both stances and movement being both ethical and unethical, suggesting that while movement is needed for encounters, including ethical encounters, movement is not in itself more or less ethical than a firm stance is.

In terms of lines of difference defined by gender identities and expressions, students moved in how they understood and experienced these identities not only in themselves but also in relation to one another. Some of the movement was in and around trans and gender-fluid communities, but some of the movement was in and around trans- and gender-fluid-ally communities. That is to say, students actively moved to become better allies to their trans and gender-fluid classmates. In these encounters, movement toward an other was ethical, whereas a stance away from an other was not. While this was the case here, this was not universally true, as evidenced in the chapter that focuses on race.

When students moved across lines of difference defined by race, there was movement in every direction. There was pushing and pulling, of ourselves and one another. There was, as is to be expected, movement away from attack, threat, and dismissal and movement toward safety, acceptance, and love. Such movement was typically but not solely within lines of difference. But there was also movement across lines of difference, like when people of color trusted their white classmates to engage in antiracist work and when white people accepted the challenge to call out and fight against racism. I understood all of this movement as ethical, but there was also unethical movement, when white people pushed people of color out or themselves away from people of color. Moreover, there were firm stances, some of which were ethical, such as when people of color stood firm with their communities, and others of which were not, such as when white people stood firm in their racism.

Crossing lines of difference defined by religious experiences was similar in that students moved away from hate and toward love but quite different in that often to move away from religious institutions that were hateful meant moving away from family who were loving. This resulted in a sort of vibrating movement, away from religion and toward family, back and forth and back and forth, which was quite wearing on young people. Here we saw young people moving between homes, as Ahmed conceptualizes them. When they had to leave one for another, they experienced loss, which I therefore understand as unethical, in contrast to the times when they could stand in both, simultaneously.

Even aside from religion, movement in relation to family experiences was complicated. As with race and religion, students moved away from family members who were ignorant, dismissive, and disrespectful, even if loving. I understand this sort of moving away from as ethical because it was in protection of their dignity. Simultaneously, though, they tried to understand their parents, in particular, thus moving closer to them, especially when their parents conveyed that they cared and were trying to understand them, too. When young people and parents tried to understand one another, there was less of a vibration and more of a give.

When movement across lines of difference allowed for such give, as distinct from forgiveness, it was consequential. It was imperative for ethical encounters. Among those of us in the course, give looked like connection, like evolving complex and nuanced understandings. It looked like intimacy. But it also looked like preparation for doing such work beyond the course, in the school, in students' families, but also in broader communities. Such moments of give rely on accepting responsibility for the harms we have done, on building trust in these particular moments, on being trustworthy, and on believing, even for just this moment, in the potential healing to come. This potential healing is a promise not just for those who have suffered but also for those who have caused the suffering, as they too are damaged in the damaging of others. It is my hope that experiencing the feeling of give, even if only in a course, might serve as an invitation to return to it, again and again.

Moving across lines of difference is not magical. It requires pushing and pulling through silence and talk. It requires agility. It requires work. Likewise, *giving*, as Ahmed (2000) conceptualizes it, is not magical. It requires the work of moving, but it also requires an openness: openness to an other, openness to connection. With openness, though, comes vulnerability: vulnerability to many things, but among them is damage. Between us, all of us, there are long histories and deep presences of damage that cannot be forgotten. Those who have survived the damages must do everything in their power to prevent their continuation. They must do everything in their power to heal. But so, too, must those who have inflicted the damages. They must take responsibility not only for what they have done but also for what they have benefited from. Without doing so, they cannot heal. And I say "they," but I mean "I" too. As a queer person, I cannot pull myself closer to someone who has inflicted pain on me and those like me, generation after generation, until that someone has learned about the damage I have endured, has learned about their role in inflicting that damage, and has earned my trust by interrupting and interrogating that damage. As a white person, I cannot expect people of color to pull close to me, as someone who has committed racist acts, even as I strive not to, and benefited from a system based on the fallacy of white supremacy, until I have learned about racism and my role in it and earned trust by interrogating and interrupting the fallacy of white supremacy. We, all of us, have to move in order to give. We have to give to have ethical encounters. This does not mean we have to move against our will. It does not mean we have to forgive. It does not mean we have to give in. But we do have to listen and learn and respond and act, ethically.

Encounters are ubiquitous. Classroom encounters are, too. But ethical encounters are not, even though they are desperately needed. Moving and giving across lines of difference, differences of consequence, can teach us to be respectful and kind, even if not comfortable, in ethical encounters, in and beyond classrooms.

Appendix

Research Methodology

This research project explored what happened when junior and senior high school students at an arts-focused charter school, which explicitly strived to create and maintain a queer-friendly context, opted to take a semester-long course focused on LGBTQ+-themed literature. The school was a public charter high school in a midsize Midwestern city. It had been founded in 2002. Since then, it had been ranked by the state department of education as effective and more recently as excellent. The school's articulated vision was to "sustain a progressive teaching and learning culture that thrives on safety, acceptance, and inclusion, rigorous academics, a commitment to the arts, and college preparedness." Building on this foundation, the school effectively achieved a reputation for recruiting students who struggled to survive as students in local public schools, particularly LGBTQ+ students. School personnel communicated an expectation that students would not act homophobically or transphobically, complementing these statements with school-wide policies and practices.

A little over three hundred students enrolled at the school during the years of this study. Approximately 56 percent received free or reduced-priced lunch, a statistic commonly used as an indicator of economically disadvantaged and impoverished students. In terms of race and ethnicity, 56 percent of students identified as white, 26 percent as African American, 10 percent as multiracial, 6 percent as Latina/o, 1 percent as Asian, and 1 percent as Pacific Islander, according to the school's demographic data. Administrators at the school estimated that 30 percent of the student population identified as LGBTQ+.

Negotiating entry to the school was facilitated by existing friendships. I had a close friend who taught at the school closer to when the school

167

first opened. Through that friend, I had come to know others who taught at the school. One current teacher at the time had become a close friend as well. Through these friendships I had come to know the principal and assistant principal. I proposed the course to them, offering to teach it for free and asking for the cost for books and the freedom to make it into a research study. They were enthusiastic about the project, so I designed the curriculum. These efforts resulted in three semester-long (eighteen-week) elective English language arts courses offered to juniors and seniors.

The course fulfilled one semester of students' English language arts requirements for those who elected to take it. I taught it three times between January 2015 and May 2016. In the first term, Ryan Schey, then a doctoral student and now a colleague and friend, joined me. (I discuss our roles more below.) The course as a whole centered on literature, including a wide range of genres and modes, representing diversity among LGBTQ+ people and characters. In response to this literature, students produced writing ranging from informal journal entries to formal essays and multimedia presentations. Each semester comprised approximately five units of study, each about a month long, and each with different focal texts and assignments (see tables 2–4). Focal texts included fiction and nonfiction, novels and short stories, and multimedia and traditional print texts. Like most if not all classes in the school, this one typically met four times weekly, with the final class session of each week being an extended double-blocked period, totaling about 240 minutes per week.

All students enrolled in the course were invited to participate in the study. None were required to do so. Among the thirty-two students who took the class, thirty-one participated in the study. (The one who did not was prohibited by her parents and repeatedly articulated her frustration.) Over the three semesters, the class became increasingly racially diverse and decreasingly diverse in terms of sexual and gender identities. To be more specific, in the first class all but one of the students identified as white, and the one biracial student was Asian and white. Among the students in the first class, there were three students who explicitly and consistently identified as gay and one who explicitly and consistently identified as trans. Moreover, there was quite a bit of experimentation and play in terms of sexuality and gender. In the third class, about half of the students identified as white and half as people of color. Only two of the ten students in this class identified as gay, and none of them identified as transgender. The two gay students, however, were experimental and playful in terms of gender expression. The second class comprised eight students. Five

Table 2. Units and related reading and writing assignments for the spring 2015 course

	Spring 2015		
Unit	Focal texts	Complementary texts	Texts created
		Book talks of a collection of LGBTQ+-themed young adult literature	
		Goodreads 2015 list of YAL with LGBT themes	
		wrapped up in books 2015 list of new releases in LGBTQ YAL	
Nonfiction *Beyond Magenta* by Kuklin (2014)		Video of Susan Kuklin talking about her work	
		Article about Leelah Alcorn's suicide	
		GLAAD Transgender 101	
		GLAAD #RealLiveTransAdult article	
		Goodreads list of YAL with trans themes	
	Collection of book reviews from the *Journal of LGBT Youth*		Individual book reviews; collective book review

continued on next page

Table 2. Continued.

	Spring 2015		
Unit	Focal texts	Complementary texts	Texts created
Memoir	Excerpt from *Mean Little Deaf Queer* by Galloway (2009)	Video of Terry Galloway talking about her work	Memoirs/autobiographies
	20 Straws: Growing Up Gay (Gjestvang & Youth Video OUTreach, 2007)		
	"It's Not Just the Aces That Are Wild" by Sedaris (2003)		
	Woodson's (2014) letter to herself in *Letter Q*		
	Excerpt from *Fun Home* by Bechdel (2006)	Video of Alison Bechdel talking about her work	
	Joe Kita article on writing memoirs	Collection of memoir resources	

Fiction	*Aristotle and Dante Discover the Secrets of the Universe* by Sáenz (2012)	Cart & Jenkins's (2006) heuristic of LGBT-themed YAL	Collections of journal entries
	Brooklyn, Burning by Brezenoff (2011)	Adichie's (2009) "The Danger of a Single Story"*	Collections of journal entries
Short Stories	"The Honorary Shepherds" by Maguire (1994)	David Hockney's 1961 painting *We Two Boys Together Clinging*	
	"Am I Blue?" by Coville (1994)		
	"My Virtual World" by Block (2009)		
	"A Word from the Nearly Distant Past" by Levithan (2009)	Mark Doty reading his poem "A Display of Mackerel"	Short stories
Essay			Argumentative essay in the form of a collective video

* This video does not relate to the unit on fiction as much as it pertains to a school event, a panel on race, that happened the day before, during the time of the fiction unit.

YAL, young adult literature.

Table 3. Units and related reading and writing assignments for the fall 2015 course

		Fall 2015	
Unit	Focal texts	Complementary texts	Texts created
History and Poetry	*Out of the Past* (film by Dupre, 1997/2005)	"I Hear America Singing" by Walt Whitman	Collections of journal entries
	Brother Outsider (film by Singer et al., 2003)	"Emily Dickinson" from *Chloe plus Olivia* (Faderman, 1995)	
		"I, Too, Sing America" and "Café: 3 AM" by Langston Hughes	
		"A Supermarket in California" and "America" by Allen Ginsberg	
		Excerpts from *I Must Resist: Bayard Rustin's Life in Letters* edited by Long (2012)	
		"Adrienne Rich: From *Twenty-One Love Poems*" from *Chloe plus Olivia* (Faderman, 1995)	
		"Audre Lorde: From *Zami: A New Spelling of My Name*" from *Chloe plus Olivia* (Faderman, 1995)	Statements of how students want to contribute to LGBTQ+ communities

Genre			
Memoir	*Beyond Magenta* by Kuklin (2014) Excerpts from *Fun Home* by Bechdel (2006)	*Some Assembly Required* by Andrews (2014) *Rethinking Normal* by Hill (2014) Excerpts from Terry Gross's (2015) interview with Bechdel, Kron, and Tesori "Ring of Keys" and "Telephone Wire" from the musical *Fun Home* by Kron & Tesori (2015) Videos of memoirs from previous students	Collections of journal entries Memoirs
Fiction	*If You Could Be Mine* by Farizan (2013) *Aristotle and Dante Discover the Secrets of the Universe* by Sáenz (2012)	"Literature from the Heart," a review of Cart & Jenkins's *The Heart Has Its Reasons*, by Greenblatt (2011) *Philadelphia* (film by Demme, 1993)	Collections of journal entries Collections of journal entries
Essay			Essays

Table 4. Units and related reading and writing assignments for the spring 2016 course

		Spring 2016	
Unit	Focal texts	Complementary texts	Texts created
History and Poetry	*Out of the Past* (film by Dupre, 1997/2005) *Brother Outsider* (film by Singer et al., 2003)	"I Hear America Singing" by Whitman and image of the author "Emily Dickinson" from *Chloe plus Olivia* (Faderman, 1995) and image of Dickinson "I, Too, Sing America" and "Café: 3 AM" by Hughes and image of the author "A Supermarket in California" and "America" by Ginsberg and image of the author Excerpts from *I Must Resist: Bayard Rustin's Life in Letters* edited by Long (2012) and image of Rustin Adrienne Rich: From *Twenty-One Love Poems* from *Chloe plus Olivia* (Faderman, 1995) and image of Rich Audre Lorde: From *Zami: A New Spelling of My Name*" from *Chloe plus Olivia* (Faderman, 1995) and image of Lorde	Collections of journal entries

	"Where Will You Be?" by Parker (1978) and image of the author Huey P. Newton's 1970 speech to the Black Panthers about gay liberation and women's liberation (BlackPast, 2018) and image of Newton		Statements of how students want to contribute to LGBTQ+ communities
Memoir	*Beyond Magenta* by Kuklin (2014) Excerpts from *Fun Home* by Bechdel (2006)	*Some Assembly Required* by Andrews (2014) Excerpts of Terry Gross's (2015) interview with Bechdel, Kron, and Tesori "Ring of Keys" and "Telephone Wire" from the musical *Fun Home* by Kron & Tesori (2015)	Collections of journal entries Memoirs
	Letters by Levithan and Woodson from *Letter Q* (2014)	Videos of memoirs from previous students	
Fiction	*If You Could Be Mine* by Farizan (2013)		Collections of journal entries

continued on next page

Table 4. Continued.

		Spring 2016	
Unit	Focal texts	Complementary texts	Texts created
Short Stories	"Trev" by Woodson (2009)		
	"Am I Blue?" by Coville (1994)		
	"My Virtual World" by Block (2009)		
	"The Honorary Shepherds" by Maguire (1994)	David Hockney's 1961 painting *We Two Boys Together Clinging*	
	"A Word from the Nearly Distant Past" by Levithan (2009)		
	"I Miss Toni" by Reed (2016; *Snap Judgment*, s nap 8)		Short stories
	"The Danger of a Single Story" by Adichie (2009)		
Essay			Essays

identified as white, and three as people of color. Their sexual identities were more varied and specific than those articulated in the other two classes: three identified as straight, one as bisexual, one as pansexual, one as fluid, one as gay, and one as asexual and homoromantic. I say all of this knowing that their identities changed throughout our time together. For that reason, when I reference a student in the book, I describe them as I experienced them in terms that matter for the featured conversation and for the particular part of the book.

Working with these young people, I tried to answer evolving research questions. I started with a broad ethnographic, what-happens-when question: What happens when junior and senior high school students at an arts-focused and queer-friendly charter school opt to take an LGBTQ+-themed literature course? There were also subquestions about the nature of the classroom context they created together, how they did so, and how they positioned themselves and one another and with what consequences. Implicit in these questions were assumed questions about how the students talked about sexual and gender identities, as well as how they talked about mutually constitutive (Winnubst, 2006) or intersecting (Crenshaw, 1991; Hill Collins, 2019) identities, like race and religion. There were also questions that I started forming while conducting the study—questions about how they talked about family, most prominently. Ultimately, I maintained the overarching question:

- What happens when junior and senior high school students at an arts-focused and queer-friendly charter school opt to take an LGBTQ+-themed literature course?

But I developed the following supporting questions, while taking David Bloome's Discourse Analysis in Education course:

- What were the students and teacher(s) in the course using their reading, writing, and talk about diverse LGBTQ+-themed literature to do?

- What were the consequences of their actions and reactions?

And these questions became more specific as I studied Ahmed:

- How were the students and teacher(s) in the course using their reading, writing, and talk about diverse LGBTQ+-themed literature to move in relation to one another?

- What were the consequences of such movement, not just among one another but among broader communities?

To answer them, I drew on a hybrid of methodologies: teacher research (Cochran-Smith & Lytle, 1993, 2009) and ethnography (Blommaert & Dong, 2020; Heath & Street, 2008). This hybridity was most evident in the first of the three semesters. In this semester, Ryan Schey accompanied me, doing coursework for a doctoral course on ethnography and a research apprenticeship, both of which I taught. He foregrounded an ethnographic participant observer role, taking field notes (Emerson et al., 2011), recording classroom interactions, and collecting course materials and student work. I adopted more of a teacher-research stance (Cochran-Smith & Lytle, 1993, 2009), taking primary responsibility for designing and implementing the curriculum, assessing student work, and interviewing students. In the second and third semesters, I assumed both sets of responsibilities. I designed and implemented curriculum, assessed student work, and interviewed students while also taking field notes, recording classroom interactions, and collecting course materials and student work. Ryan, however, continued on the project as a research assistant, organizing the data I constructed.

All things considered, like snow days and senior internships, I taught and studied 187 days. Of these, 75 percent were single blocks of just under fifty minutes, and the remaining 25 percent were double blocks of about ninety minutes. All 187 days were documented with field notes and the collection of course materials and student work. In the first term, Ryan took very detailed field notes during and after class. In the second and third terms, I took anecdotal records during class and developed them into field notes (Hubbard et al., 1993), usually in my car in the parking lot after class.

As I developed rapport with students, I felt more comfortable asking their permission to record our class discussions. In the earlier days of each term, I would ask to record audio. As we got to know one another better, I would ask to record video. In the first two terms this was prompted by students' presentations at the conclusion of the first units. In the third term it was prompted by a particularly invigorating conversation. Ultimately, thirty-three classes were audio recorded and 106 were video recorded. These were all indexed by Ryan.

Interviews were also conducted at the start and end of each term. Overall, I conducted twenty-eight introductory student interviews, Ryan conducted one, and two participants were not interviewed at the start of their semesters. These interviews were somewhat structured. In the early interviews of the final term, Jenna and Khalil asked to be interviewed together, and they were. Overall, I conducted twenty-two concluding student interviews, and seven student participants were not interviewed at the end of their semesters. I did not conduct concluding interviews with the two students who did not interview initially. When students were not interviewed, it seemed to be because we could not find a time that would work; the semester always seemed busier toward the end, as exams, internships, and graduation were priorities. The interviews comprised mostly follow-up questions based on our semester together. Some of the questions were for all student participants, but others were completely individualized. Again, Jenna and Khalil were interviewed together. Surprisingly, to me, they brought along their close friend. She stayed and participated in the interview, but because she never returned the consent form I gave her I excluded her words from the data set. The only two students who were not interviewed initially asked to be interviewed together at the close of the term, and I welcomed the opportunity. In addition to the student participant interviews, several staff interviews were conducted at the end of the first term as a part of a video project Ryan and I were doing with the juniors, since the seniors were doing internships. Ryan conducted one of these, and Parker conducted three more. All of the fifty-five interviews were audio recorded and transcribed.

Ryan organized these data, including field notes, course materials, student work, interview recordings and transcripts, audio and video recordings, and indexes. He organized them chronologically so that each class was represented by all of the data for that day. He did this for all three semesters.

In the summer of 2015, Ryan and I listened to and watched, together, the forty-six recordings to identify events for transcription. At this point, "events" was loosely defined, drawing on our regular engagement with literacy events (Heath, 1983; Street, 1999). In the summer of 2016, I reviewed the ninety-three recordings and their indexes to select events for transcription. Among these transcripts, I selected 210 events for transcription. They represented 112 days of class. Some days are represented multiple times and others not at all. I removed six events that no longer seemed pertinent to the study. That left 204 in the data set. These processes—conducting field work, collecting or constructing data, and organizing data—are all always interpretive and therefore analytic, but the more explicit methods of analysis were conducted on this data set.

I coded the transcripts of the classroom discussions iteratively and recursively, in a constant comparative method (Heath & Street, 2008). Codes sometimes broke into more codes, other times collapsed into one another, and still other times dissipated all together. When I recoded the complete data set, I worked with fourteen codes. As I started clustering the events into codes, I revised them to eleven codes. Seven of these focused on mutually constitutive (Winnubst, 2006) or intersecting (Crenshaw, 1991; Hill Collins, 2019) identities: race, class, sexuality and gender, religion, linguistic diversity, immigration status and experiences, and mental health and illness. Four focused on themes such as family, internalized hatred, violence, and vulnerability. Working with these, I created three tables that became integral to my analysis:

1. First, I created a table of all transcribed events and a brief description of the discussion represented in each. I noted, on this table, the discussions that I found particularly compelling. These were 39 of the 204.

2. The next table I created was one of all transcribed events and the codes found within. I noted, on this table, codes that seemed particularly pronounced in events. At this point, there were eleven codes.

3. Finally, I created a table comprising events that I noted as compelling and organized them into categories by the pronounced codes in them. I included events that I understood as central to the categories as well as those I understood as peripheral.

This third table was my guide for the next step in my analysis, in which I created a document for each central event on the table. By this time, I was just starting to understand the events as encounters, as I define in the introduction of this book.

I called these documents prewrites. I titled each with the overarching theme—that is, how it was organized in the third table; the date of the encounter represented; a brief title for the encounter; and the codes represented in the encounter. Each goes on to describe the encounter, to list the speakers in the encounter, to discuss analytic points I considered while drafting, and to include the transcript of the encounter. When I finished creating the cluster of prewrites on any given code, as represented on the third table, I wrote a memo (Glaser, 1978) trying to move myself toward the argument I was trying to make with that particular code.

As I created these documents, both the prewrites and the memos, I drafted and revised the codes and their order. In doing so, I began to craft my argument. As I was doing this, I would sometimes realize that certain encounters belonged in other categories, and I would move them where they belonged. I made peace with some encounters belonging in multiple categories. Sometimes, as I started to shape my arguments, I would realize that a central encounter really was becoming more peripheral, and vice versa. I would move them accordingly. Other times, I would remember an encounter that was missing from a theme, and I would search for it and add it. In this way, sometimes encounters that I had not initially noted as compelling would be pulled in, and vice versa. All of this was iterative and recursive. Throughout this, I revised and refined the categories.

Then, I went through the third table, prewrites, and memos. I paid attention to peripheral stories in earlier themes. Then I perused all encounters with the code that led to the theme to see whether the argument held, fell apart, or got more complicated. I added and deleted encounters as appropriate. I went through field notes, too, to identify pertinent encounters that were not transcribed. Throughout this process, I kept revising categories in relationship to one another. For example, I separated *sexuality* and *gender* into two separate categories and moved some of *internalized hatred* into the *sexuality* category and some of it into the *race* category. Violence was in many ways about internalized hatred, so when I moved that part to *sexuality*, the *violence* category was insubstantial, particularly since I made the decision not to share some stories of violence to avoid positioning my students as victims. I merged *linguistic diversity* and *immigration status and experiences* because the two were so intertwined, and I ultimately excluded them from this book because they demand analysis beyond the focus of this book. I also pulled the *class* and *mental health and illness* categories because they were less substantial, not because they were less important. Finally, it turned out that vulnerability was woven throughout all of the categories more than being a stand-alone one.

In shifting to writing, I first focused on one category at a time. I read and reread the prewrites. I organized and reorganized them. I identified all complementary data, like course materials, student work, and interview transcripts, that I needed to be able to tell the stories. Working across data sources allowed me to triangulate my findings. Then I wrote, category by category, chapter by chapter. I also organized and reorganized the resulting chapters as my argument developed. This eventually brought me to the organizational structure of the book as you see it.

After all of the chapters were drafted and organized, I went through the whole and identified each encounter and the people involved in it. Then I looked closely at how those people move in that encounter—when people moved, from where and to where, and why. I considered where they were in relation to others and with what consequences. I drew on Ahmed to reflect on the past encounters that informed the focal one and to imagine the potential future encounters that the focal one could open up. I wrote about these considerations and reflections after each encounter. Not surprisingly, it turns out the encounters cannot be dichotomized into those where there is movement and those where there is not; sometimes there is just a little teetering, for example, and sometimes the provocation for moving matters, whether it is a pushing or pulling, and who is doing the provoking. Sometimes there is just a little "give," to use Ahmed's word. I tried to represent that complexity in my writing. Then, at the end of each chapter, I studied the collection of encounters to explore the idea of ethical versus unethical, that is, to make some judgment about which of the encounters I understood as ethical and which I did not and why, again drawing on Ahmed. Again, not surprisingly, it turns out the movement, or even the stances, cannot be dichotomized into ethical and unethical, at least not only. Often it is more complicated than that. I tried to represent that complexity in my writing.

Throughout this process, I had several people read the report in part or in whole. Most significantly, several of these readers were students represented in the report. Whether they read parts or the whole, they tended to focus on the sections that represented them. They provided feedback on my representation and interpretation. Their feedback was invaluable. As is typical in ethnographic research, this analytic process was much messier and much less linear than this description conveys (Blommaert & Dong, 2020); still, it was systematic and intentional (Cochran-Smith & Lytle, 1993).

The entire study was shaped by the fact that I identify as a white, queer, cis woman. In keeping with Blommaert and Dong's (2020) notion of ethnography as "necessarily critical and counter-hegemonic" (p. 10), I strove to interrogate and dismantle oppressive power relations. In an effort to do so, in and beyond the context of this study, I have worked diligently to acknowledge my privileges, discover related blind spots, and educate myself in ways that compensate for my experiential and epistemological shortcomings defined by my whiteness and cisgender identity, in particular. I understand this as lifelong work and recognize that in this study I am, as always, in process. This is my limitation; this is a limitation of the researcher.

There are other limitations defined by the study's design. Ethnographies, while stellar at providing complexity and nuance, do not even strive for generalizability. This is also true for teacher research. Further, teacher research is tied tightly to the focal pedagogy and curriculum, as it is in this study, and pedagogy and curriculum are, ideally, deeply human and therefore never uniform, much less perfect. This is the nature of documenting practice. So, the accounts I share are not images of perfect teaching. They are just teaching. Real teaching, shaped by innumerable decisions made in split seconds with and among a group of adolescents within the constraints of the institution of schooling. This is a limitation of the research.

In other words, this study, like any study, is limited. Its limitations are why your study is needed: to supplement, complement, even debunk this and other studies. None of them stand alone. None of them do it all. They work together to helps us make sense of one another, to make sense of ourselves, so that we might encounter one another, move closer to one another, ethically.

References

Adichie, C. N. (2009, July). *The danger of a single story* [Video]. TED Conferences. https://www.ted.com/talks/chimamanda_ngozi_adichie_the_danger_of_a_single_story

Ahmed, S. (2000). *Strange encounters: Embodied others in post-coloniality.* Routledge.

Ahmed, S. (2010). *The promise of happiness.* Duke University Press.

Ahmed, S. (2012). *On being included: Racism and diversity in institutional life.* Duke University Press.

Ahmed, S. (2014). *The cultural politics of emotion* (2nd ed.). Edinburgh University Press.

Ahmed, S. (2021). Travelling with strangers. *Journal of Intercultural Studies,* 42(1), 8–23.

Airton, L., & Meyer, E. J. (2018). Glossary of terms. In E. J. Meyer & A. Pullen Sanfacon (Eds.), *Supporting transgender and gender creative youth: Schools, families, and communities in action* (revised ed., pp. 315–324). Peter Lang.

Alexander, J. (2008). *Literacy, sexuality, pedagogy: Theory and practice for composition studies.* Utah State University Press.

Andrews, A. (2014). *Some assembly required: The not-so-secret life of a transgender teen.* Simon & Schuster.

Athanases, S. (1996). A gay-themed lesson in an ethnic literature curriculum: Tenth graders' responses to "Dear Anita." *Harvard Educational Review,* 66(2), 231–256.

Atkinson, E., & DePalma, R. (2009). Un-believing the matrix: Queering consensual heteronormativity. *Gender and Education,* 21(1), 17–29.

Aukerman, M. (2021). Listening across differences. In D. Sumara & D. E. Alvermann (Eds.), *Ideas that changed literacy practices: First-person accounts from leading voices* (pp. 35–43). Myers Education Press.

Bechdel, A. (2006). *Fun home: A family tragicomic.* Mariner Books.

Bittner, R. (2018). Queer Christian voices in YA literature: A scholar's account of #OwnVoices positioning in the 21st century. *Research on Diversity in Youth Literature,* 1(1), Article 5.

Blackburn, M. V. (2002/2003). Disrupting the (hetero)normative: Exploring literacy performances and identity work with queer youth. *Journal of Adolescent & Adult Literacy*, *46*(4), 312–324.

Blackburn, M. (2003a). Exploring literacy performances and power dynamics at The Loft: Queer youth reading the world and the word. *Research in the Teaching of English*, *37*, 467–490.

Blackburn, M. V. (2003b). Losing, finding, and making space for activism through literacy performances and identity work. *Penn GSE Perspectives on Urban Education*, *2*(1). https://urbanedjournal.gse.upenn.edu/archive/volume-2-issue-1-spring-2003/losing-finding-and-making-space-activism-through-literacy-perfo

Blackburn, M. V. (2005a). Agency in borderland discourses: Examining language use in a community center with Black queer youth. *Teachers College Record*, *107*(1), 89–113.

Blackburn, M. V. (2005b). Co-constructing space for literacy and identity work with LGBTQ youth. *Afterschool Matters*, (4), 17–23.

Blackburn, M. V. (2019). Literacy teaching and learning in school as polyphonic: A close examination of a lesson focused on *Fun home*, the graphic memoir and musical. In D. Bloome, M. L. Castanheira, C. Leung, & J. Rowsell (Eds.), *Re-theorizing literacy practices: Complex social and cultural contexts* (pp. 115–125). Routledge.

Blackburn, M. V. (2021). Pedagogy and pleasure: Trans and gender transgressive students in an LGBTQ-themed literature class. *Pedagogy, Culture & Society*, *29*(5), 773–791. https://doi.org/10.1080/14681366.2021.1912161

Blackburn, M. V., & Clark, C. T. (2011). Analyzing talk in a long-term literature discussion group: Ways of operating within LGBT-inclusive and queer discourses. *Reading Research Quarterly*, *46*(3), 222–248.

Blackburn, M. V., Clark, C. T., & Nemeth, E. A. (2015). Examining queer elements and ideologies in LGBT-themed literature: What queer literature can offer young adult readers. *Journal of Literacy Research*, *47*(1), 11–48.

Blackburn, M. V., & Deiri, Y. (2018). Exploring sexuality, gender, nationality, and religion through Sara Farizan's *If You Could Be Mine*. In P. Greathouse, B. Eisenbach, & J. F. Kaywell (Eds.), *Queer adolescent literature as a complement to the English language arts curriculum* (pp. 51–60). Rowan & Littlefield.

Blackburn, M. V., & Pennell, S. M. (2018). Teaching students to question assumptions about gender and sexuality. *Phi Delta Kappan*, *100*(2), 27–31. https://doi.org/10.1177/0031721718803566

Blackburn, M. V., & Schey, R. (2017). Adolescent literacies beyond heterosexual hegemony. In K. A. Hinchman & D. A. Appleman (Eds.), *Adolescent literacy: A handbook of practice-based research* (pp. 38–60). Guilford Press.

Blackburn, M. V., & Schey, R. (2018). Shared vulnerability, collaborative composition, and the interrogation and reification of oppressive values in a high school LGBTQ-themed literature course. *Journal of Literacy Research, 50*(3), 335–358. https://doi.org/10.1177/1086296X18784336

BlackPast. (2012, November 16). *(1977)* The Combahee River Collective statement: *Primary document.* https://www.blackpast.org/african-american-history/combahee-river-collective-statement-1977/

BlackPast. (2018, April 17). *(1970) Huey P. Newton, "The women's liberation and gay liberation movements."* https://www.blackpast.org/african-american-history/speeches-african-american-history/huey-p-newton-women-s-liberation-and-gay-liberation-movements/

Blazar, D. (2009). Self-discovery through character connections: Opening up to gayness in *Angels in America. English Journal, 98*(4), 77–84.

Block, F. L. (2009). My virtual world. In M. Cart (Ed.), *How beautiful the ordinary: Twelve stories of identity* (pp. 73–92). HarperTeen.

Blommaert, J., & Dong, J. (2020). *Ethnographic fieldwork: A beginner's guide* (2nd ed.). Multilingual Matters.

Botelho, M. J., & Rudman, M. K. (2009). *Critical multicultural analysis of children's literature: Mirrors, windows, and doors.* Routledge.

Brezenoff, S. (2011). *Brooklyn, burning.* Carolrhoda Lab.

Bryson, M., & de Castell, S. (1993). Queer pedagogy: Praxis makes im/perfect. *Canadian Journal of Education / Revue canadienne de l'éducation, 18*(3), 285–305. https://doi.org/10.2307/1495388

Burack, C. (2014). *Tough love: Sexuality, compassion, and the Christian right.* State University of New York Press.

Buys, R., & Marotta, V. (2021). Relational theories of encounters and the relational subject. *Journal of Intercultural Studies, 42*(1), 99–113. https://doi.org/10.1080/07256868.2020.1864968

Carey-Webb, A. (2001). *Literature and lives: A response-based, cultural studies approach to teaching English.* National Council of Teachers of English.

Cart, M., & Jenkins, C. A. (2006). *The heart has its reasons: Young adult literature with gay/lesbian/queer content, 1969–2004.* Scarecrow Press.

Clark, C. T., & Blackburn, M. V. (2009). Reading LGBT-themed literature with young people: What's possible? *English Journal, 98*(4), 25–32.

Coates, T.-N. (2015). *Between the world and me.* One World.

Cochran-Smith, M., & Lytle, S. L. (1993). *Inside/outside: Teacher research and knowledge.* Teachers College Press.

Cochran-Smith, M., & Lytle, S. L. (2009). *Inquiry as stance: Practitioner research for the next generation.* Teachers College Press.

Coville, B. (1994). Am I blue? In M. D. Bauer (Ed.), *Am I blue? Coming out from the silence* (pp. 1–18). HarperTrophy.

Crenshaw, K. (1991). Mapping the margins: Identity politics, intersectionality, and violence against women of color. *Stanford Law Review, 43*(6), 1241–1299.

Crockett, E. (2017, March 15). The controversy over Chimamanda Ngozi Adichie and trans women, explained. *Vox.* https://www.vox.com/identities/2017/3/15/14910900/chimamanda-ngozi-adichie-transgender-women-comments-apology

Cruz, C. (2013). LGBTQ youth of color video making as radical curriculum: A brother mourning his brother and a theory in the flesh. *Curriculum Inquiry,* 43(4), 441–460.

de Castell, S., & Jenson, J. (2007). No place like home: Sexuality, community, and identity among street-involved queer and questioning youth. In M. V. Blackburn & C. T. Clark (Eds.), *Literacy research for political action and social change* (pp. 131–152). Peter Lang.

Demme, J. (Director). (1993). *Philadelphia* [Film]. TriStar Pictures.

DesPrez, E., Baca, D., Blackburn, M., Chen, A., Coles, J. A., Dominguez, M., ife, f., Pennell, S. M., & Shelton, S. A. (2018, October 25). *Statement on gender and language.* National Council of Teachers of English. https://ncte.org/statement/genderfairuseoflang/

Doty, M. (2011). A Display of mackerel. In PBS NewsHour. PBS. https://www.pbs.org/video/pbs-newshour-poet-mark-doty-reads-a-display-of-mackerel/

Dupre, J. (Director & Producer). (1997/2005). *Out of the past: The struggle for gay and lesbian rights in America* [DVD]. Allumination.

Emerson, R. M., Fretz, R. I., & Shaw, L. L. (2011). *Writing ethnographic fieldnotes* (2nd ed.). University of Chicago Press.

Epstein, D. (2000). Reading gender, reading sexualities: Children and the negotiation of meaning in "alternative" texts. In W. J. Spurlin (Ed.), *Lesbian and gay studies and the teaching of English: Positions, pedagogies, and cultural politics* (pp. 213–233). National Council of Teachers of English.

Faderman, L. (1995). *Chloe plus Olivia: An anthology of lesbian literature from the seventeenth century to the present.* Penguin Books.

Farizan, S. (2013). *If you could be mine.* Algonquin Young Readers.

Galloway, T. (2009). *Mean little deaf queer: A memoir.* Beacon Press.

Gjestvang, L. (Director), & Youth Video OUTreach. (2007). *20 straws: Growing up gay* [Film]. Youth Video OUTreach.

Glaser, B. G. (1978). *Theoretical sensitivity: Advances in the methodology of grounded theory.* Sociology Press.

Gonçalves, Z. M. (2005). *Sexuality and the politics of ethos in the writing classroom.* Southern Illinois University Press.

Gonzales, J. (2010). Risk and threat in critical inquiry: Vacancies, violations, and vacuums. In M. V. Blackburn, C. T. Clark, L. M. Kenney, & J. M. Smith (Eds.), *Acting out!: Combating homophobia through teacher activism* (pp. 74–87). Teachers College Press.

Green, K. M. (2016). Troubling the waters: Mobilizing a trans* analytic. In E. P. Johnson (Ed.), *No tea, no shade: New writings in Black queer studies* (pp. 65–82). Duke University Press.

Greenbaum, V. (1994). Literature out of the closet: Bringing gay and lesbian texts and subtexts out in high school English. *English Journal, 83*(5), 71–74.

Greenblatt, E. (2011). Literature from the heart. *Journal of LGBT Youth, 8*(1), 99–102.

Gross, T. (Host). (2015, August 17). Alison Bechdel & songwriters on 'Fun home' musical [Radio broadcast interview]. *Fresh air.* NPR / WHYY. https://www.npr.org/2015/08/24/432622572/alison-bechdel-songwriters-on-fun-home-musical

Halverson, E. R. (2007). Listening to the voices of queer youth: The dramaturgical process as identity exploration. In M. V. Blackburn & C. T. Clark (Eds.), *Literacy research for political action and social change* (pp. 153–175). Peter Lang.

Hamilton, G. (1998). Reading *Jack. English Education, 30*(1), 24–39.

Heath, S. B. (1983). *Ways with words: Language, life, and work in communities and classrooms.* Cambridge University Press.

Heath, S. B., & Street, B. V. (2008). *On ethnography: Approaches to language and literacy research.* Teachers College Press.

Helmer, K. (2015). *Reading queerly in the high school classroom: Exploring a gay and lesbian literature course* [Doctoral dissertation, University of Massachusetts Amherst]. ScholarWorks@UMass Amherst, 366. https://doi.org/10.7275/6858577.0

Helmer, K. (2016a). Gay and lesbian literature disrupting the heteronormative space of the high school English classroom. *Sex Education, 16*(1), 35–48.

Helmer, K. (2016b). Queer literacies: A multidimensional approach to reading LGBTQ-themed literature. In D. Linville & D. L. Carlson (Eds.), *Beyond borders: Queer eros and ethos (ethics) in LGBTQ young adult literature* (pp. 181–198). Peter Lang.

Hill, K. R. (2014). *Rethinking normal: A memoir in transition.* Simon & Schuster.

Hill Collins, P. (2019). *Intersectionality as critical social theory.* Duke University Press.

Hoffman, M. (1993). Teaching *Torch song*: Gay literature in the classroom. *English Journal, 82*(5), 55–58.

Hubbard, R., Shagoury, R., & Power, B. M. (1993). *The art of classroom inquiry: A handbook for teacher-researchers.* Pearson Education.

Kendi, I. X. (2016). *Stamped from the beginning: The definitive history of racist ideas in America.* Nation Books.

Kendi, I. X. (2019). *How to be an antiracist.* One World.

Kenney, L. M. (2010). Being out and reading queer-inclusive texts in a high school English classroom. In M. V. Blackburn, C. T. Clark, L. M. Kenney, & J. M. Smith (Eds.), *Acting out!: Combating homophobia through teacher activism* (pp. 56–73). Teachers College Press.

Kohan, J. (2013–2019). *Orange is the new black* [TV series]. Lionsgate Films; Netflix.

Kron, L. (Lyricist), & Tesori, J. (Composer). (2015). *Fun home: A new Broadway musical* [Album]. PS Classics.

Kuklin, S. (2014). *Beyond magenta: Transgender teens speak out.* Candlewick Press.

Kumashiro, K. K. (2001). "Posts" perspectives on anti-oppressive education in social studies, English, mathematics, and science classrooms. *Educational Researcher, 30*(3), 3–12.

Levithan, D. (2009). A word from the nearly distant past. In M. Cart (Ed.), *How beautiful the ordinary: Twelve stories of identity* (pp. 7–22). HarperTeen.

Levithan, D. (2014). David Levithan. In S. Moon (Ed.), *The letter Q: Queer writers' notes to their younger selves* (pp. 24–28). Scholastic.

Linville, D., & Carlson, D. L. (Eds.). (2016). *Beyond borders: Queer eros and ethos (ethics) in LGBTQ young adult literature*. Peter Lang.

Long, M. G. (Ed.). (2012). *I must resist: Bayard Rustin's life in letters*. City Lights Books.

Lovaas, K. E., Elia, J. P., & Yep, G. A. (2006). Shifting ground(s): Surveying the contested terrain of LGBT studies and queer theory. In K. E. Lovaas, J. P. Elia, & G. A. Yep (Eds.), *LGBT studies and queer theory: New conflicts, collaborations, and contested terrain* (pp. 1–18). Harrington Park Press.

Love, B. L. (2019). *We want to do more than survive: Abolitionist teaching and the pursuit of educational freedom*. Beacon Press.

Maguire, G. (1994). The honorary shepherds. In M. D. Bauer (Ed.), *Am I blue? Coming out from the silence* (pp. 63–84). HarperTrophy.

Miller, s. (2019). *About gender identity justice in schools and communities*. Teachers College Press.

Miller, s. (2020). Working through concerns and fears: Tips for communicating and messaging about gender identity complexity for cisgender people. In J. Green, R. A. Hoskin, C. Mayo, & s. Miller, *Navigating trans*++ *and complex gender identities* (pp. 19–78). Bloomsbury Academic.

Moita-Lopes, L. P. (2006). Queering literacy teaching: Analyzing gay-themed discourses in a fifth-grade class in Brazil. *Journal of Language, Identity & Education, 5*(1), 31–50.

Muñoz, J. E. (2000). Feeling brown: Ethnicity and affect in Ricardo Bracho's *The sweetest hangover (and other STDs)*. *Theatre Journal, 52*(1), 67–79.

National Center for Transgender Equality. (2016). *Understanding transgender people: The basics*. https://transequality.org/issues/resources/understanding-transgender-people-the-basics

Omi, M., & Winant, H. (2014). *Racial formation in the United States* (3rd ed.). Routledge.

Parker, P. (1978). Where will you be? *Webpages@SCU*. https://webpages.scu.edu/ftp/lgarber/courses/eng67F10texts/ParkerWhereWillYouBe.pdf

Pierce, C. (1970). Offensive mechanisms. In F. B. Barbour (Ed.), *The Black seventies* (pp. 265–282). Porter Sargent.

Reed, D. (2016). I miss Toni [Podcast episode]. In G. Washington (Host), *Snap judgment*. NPR.

Reese, J. (1998). Teaching tolerance through literature: Dealing with issues of homosexuality in English class. *The International Schools Journal, 17*(2), 35–40.

Ryan, C. L., & Hermann-Wilmarth, J. M. (2018). *Reading the rainbow: LGBTQ-inclusive literacy instruction in the elementary classroom.* Teachers College Press.

Sáenz, B. A. (2012). *Aritstotle and Dante discover the secrets of the universe.* Simon & Schuster.

Schall, J., & Kauffmann, G. (2003). Exploring literature with gay and lesbian characters in the elementary school. *Journal of Children's Literature, 29*(1), 36–45.

Schey, R., & Blackburn, M. V. (2019a). "The fact of a doorframe": Adolescents finding pleasure in transgender-themed YAL. *The ALAN Review, 47*(1), 29–40.

Schey, R., & Blackburn, M. (2019b). Queer ruptures to normative literacy practices: Toward visualizing, hypothesizing, and empathizing. *Research in the Teaching of English, 54*(1), 58–80.

Schey, R., & Uppstrom, A. (2010). Activist work as entry-year teachers: What we've learned. In M. V. Blackburn, C. T. Clark, L. M. Kenney, & J. M. Smith (Eds.), *Acting out!: Combating homophobia through teacher activism* (pp. 88–102). Teachers College Press.

Sedaris, D. (2003, June 20). It's not just the aces that are wild. In I. Glass (Host), *I'm in charge now* (No. 240, Act 1) [Audio podcast episode], *This American life*. NPR.

Serano, J. (2016a). *Outspoken: A decade of transgender activism and trans feminism.* Switch Hitter Press.

Serano, J. (2016b). *Whipping girl: A transsexual woman on sexism and the scapegoating of femininity.* Seal Press.

Sims Bishop, R. (1990). Mirrors, windows, and sliding glass doors. *Perspectives: Choosing and Using Books for the Classroom, 6*(3), ix–xi.

Simon, R., hicks, b. l., Walkland, T., Gallagher, B., Evis, S., & Baer, P. (2018). "But in the end, you are all beautiful": Exploring gender through digital composition. *English Journal, 107*(3), 39–46.

Sims, R. (1982). *Shadow and substance: Afro-American experience in contemporary children's fiction.* National Council of Teachers of English.

Singer, B. (Producer & Director), Kates, N. D. (Producer & Director), & Chandra, M. (Co-producer). (2003). *Brother outsider: The life of Bayard Rustin.* Question Why Films.

Soloway, J. (2014–2019). *Transparent* [TV series]. Amazon Studios.

Street, B. V. (1999). The meanings of literacy. In D. A. Wagner, R. L. Venezky, & B. V. Street (Eds.), *Literacy: An international handbook.* Westview Press.

Thein, A. H., & Kedley, K. E. (2016). Out of the closet and all grown up: Problematizing normative narratives of coming-out and coming-of-age in young adult literature. In D. Linville & D. L. Carlson (Eds.), *Beyond borders: Queer eros and ethos (ethics) in LGBTQ young adult literature.* Peter Lang.

Vetter, A. M. (2010). "'Cause I'm a G": Identity work of a lesbian teen in language arts. *Journal of Adolescent & Adult Literacy, 54*(2), 98–108.

Waite, S. (2017). *Teaching queer: Radical possibilities for writing and knowing.* University of Pittsburgh Press.

Winnubst, S. (2006). *Queering freedom*. Indiana University Press.

Woodson, J. (2009). Trev. In M. Cart (Ed.), *How beautiful the ordinary: Twelve stories of identity* (pp. 63–72). HarperTeen.

Woodson, J. (2014). Jacqueline Woodson. In S. Moon (Ed., with J. Lecesne), *The letter Q: Queer writers' notes to their younger selves* (pp. 16–18). Scholastic.

Index

agility, 3, 11, 78, 111, 149, 161, 164, 166
"Am I Blue?," 42, 48
antiracist, 79, 80, 81
Aristotle and Dante Discover the Secrets of the Universe, 1, 28–30, 35–36, 46, 47–48, 50, 82, 92–96, 145, 155
asexuality, 36–39, 115
attraction, 10

Beyond Magenta, 64, 65–66, 142, 145–146, 153, 158
bisexual, 38, 122, 138–139
Bloome, David 177
Brooklyn, Burning, 1, 59, 62–63, 82, 151

Christian Right, 114–116, 116–117, 119, 121–122, 123–124
coming out, 28–34, 40–41, 49, 73, 116–117, 121–1222, 128, 129, 137, 139, 143, 152, 157
conditional cis privilege, 39
curricular inclusion, 12, 164

dialogue, 5–6, 19
differences, 3, 5–6, 8–9, 12

encounters
  antiracist, 82, 88, 91, 97, 104, 105, 110

ethical, 3, 3–7, 10–11, 25, 157, 160–2, 164, 165, 166
  future, 4, 34, 56, 59, 86, 108, 125, 182
  generous, 5
  unethical, 5, 34, 125
ethical, 7, 11, 19, 24, 182, 183
  classrooms, 19
  encounters, 3, 3–7, 10–11, 25, 157, 160–2, 164, 165, 166
  movement, 11, 51, 78, 110, 125, 148–9, 165
ethnography 13–14, 177–178, 182, 183
externalizing internalized hatred, 44–49, 157

firm stances, 11, 24, 109, 160, 164, 165
forgiving, 25, 151–7, 161, 166
Fun Home, 128

gender identity, 53–54
gender-fluid, 59–64, 65–69, 70, 74, 146, 164
give, 6, 11, 13, 109, 111, 153, 157, 159, 160, 161, 165–6, 182
giving, 10–11, 25, 155–6, 157–160, 160–162, 166

historicity, 4, 107, 154, 160–161

home, 5, 7–8, 104, 116
homoromantic, 38, 40, 115, 140
heuristic of LGBT-themed young
    adult literature, 12, 163

identities
    interlocking, 5(n)
    intersectional, 5(n), 12, 177, 180
    multiple and variable, 8–9
    mutually constitutive, 5(n), 25, 177,
        180
ideological movement, 9–10
If You Could Be Mine, 21, 44–46,
    55–58, 118, 145
internalized hatred, 44–51, 54, 128,
    129, 157
interrogating normal, 64–65, 108, 166,
    182
intimate responsibility, 7

labels, 34–44, 80, 153
LGBT studies and queer studies,
    27–28, 34
LGBTQ-themed literature in
    secondary classrooms, 11–13
lines of difference, 129, 132, 164–166
listening, 6–7, 10, 19, 109, 149, 160, 166

masculine men, 49, 55, 75–78
McCready, Lance, 83
microaggressions, 108(n)
movement toward, 7–9, 62, 89, 143,
    145, 148, 160, 164
movement within, 9–11
Muslim, 21, 113–115, 117–118, 125

National Center for Transgender
    Equality, 54
National Council of Teachers of
    English's *Statement on Gender
    and Language*, 145(n)

Newton, Huey P., 83

off-white, 86
ossification, 13, 51, 78, 111, 161, 164

pansexual, 38–39, 39–40, 72, 120
people who imagine themselves to be
    white, 80, 81

questioning, 20, 48, 66, 67, 68, 122

race, 79–80, 91
racism, 80, 106
racist, 80, 100, 104
race and ethnicity, 92
repulsion, 10
researcher positionality, 24, 182–183
respectful distance, 6
Rethinking Normal, 69, 129–30

sacrifice, 119–122, 124
Schey, Ryan, 14(n), 23, 168, 178
sex, gender, sexuality, and sexual
    behavior, 28
Some Assembly Required, 55, 69, 76,
    116, 129–130, 132, 145
strangers, 7–8

teacher research, 14, 23–24, 178, 183
trans allies, 55–59, 70, 71, 74, 78
trans communities, 69–71, 74–75
trans-exclusionary radical feminism,
    163(n)

unethical, 5, 24, 34, 49, 78, 110, 125,
    156, 165, 182
unforgivable, 161

whiteness, 82, 92, 104, 107

www.ingramcontent.com/pod-product-compliance
Lightning Source LLC
Chambersburg PA
CBHW030331270326
41926CB00010B/1578